Entrepreneurial Excellence

Proven Methods to Build and Grow a Thriving Business

HUBERT MILLS

The presentation of the information is without contract or any type of guarantee assurance. The trademarks that are used are without any consent, and the publication of the trademark is without permission or backing by the trademark owner. All trademarks and brands within this book are for clarifying purposes only and are the owned by the owners themselves, not affiliated with this document.

Table of Contents

Chapter 1.. 6

Introduction to Entrepreneurial Excellence 6

Defining Entrepreneurship 6

The Mindset of a Successful Entrepreneur 11

Common Myths About Entrepreneurship 16

Benefits and Challenges of Being an Entrepreneur
.... 21

Setting Your Entrepreneurial Goals 26

Chapter 2 31

Identifying Business Opportunities 31

Understanding Market Needs 31

Evaluating Business Ideas 36

Conducting Feasibility Studies 42

Identifying Niche Markets............................... 47

Using SWOT Analysis to Assess Opportunities 52

Chapter 3 57

Crafting a Winning Business Plan 57

Components of a Business Plan 57

Market Research and Analysis 62

Financial Projections and Budgeting 68

Strategic Planning... 73

Presenting Your Business Plan to Investors 80

Chapter 4 85

Building Your Brand and Marketing Strategy 85

Defining Your Brand Identity................................ 85

Creating a Unique Value Proposition.................... 90

Developing a Marketing Plan 95

Leveraging Digital Marketing.............................. 101

Building Customer Loyalty..................................106

Chapter 1

Introduction to Entrepreneurial Excellence

Defining Entrepreneurship

Entrepreneurship is a dynamic and multifaceted concept that has been the driving force behind innovation, economic growth, and societal change. It is more than just starting a business; it is about identifying opportunities, taking risks, and leveraging resources to create value. Entrepreneurs are the catalysts of change, pushing boundaries, and challenging the status quo. This chapter delves into the essence of entrepreneurship, providing a comprehensive understanding of what it means to be an entrepreneur.

At its core, entrepreneurship involves the creation, development, and management of a business venture with the aim of making a profit. However, this definition barely scratches the surface of what it truly entails. Entrepreneurship is a way of thinking, a mindset that embraces change, innovation, and a relentless pursuit of improvement. It is about seeing possibilities where others see obstacles and having the courage to act on those possibilities despite the risks involved.

A successful entrepreneur possesses a distinctive mindset characterized by creativity, resilience, and a strong sense of purpose. Creativity is essential as it allows entrepreneurs to develop unique solutions to problems and to differentiate their offerings in a crowded marketplace. It involves thinking outside the box and being willing to experiment and learn from failure. Resilience is equally important because the entrepreneurial journey is fraught with challenges and setbacks. Entrepreneurs must be able to bounce back from failures, learn from their mistakes, and keep moving forward. A strong sense of purpose drives entrepreneurs to persevere through tough times and stay committed to their vision.

One common myth about entrepreneurship is that it is a path to quick riches. While there are certainly stories of entrepreneurs who have achieved significant financial success, the reality is that entrepreneurship often involves long hours, hard work, and financial uncertainty. Many entrepreneurs face significant challenges and failures before achieving success. It is crucial to approach entrepreneurship with realistic expectations and an understanding that it is a marathon, not a sprint. Success requires persistence, patience, and a willingness to learn and adapt.

Another myth is that entrepreneurs are born, not made. While some individuals may have innate qualities that lend themselves to entrepreneurship, such as risk tolerance and creativity, many entrepreneurial skills can be developed and honed over time. Education, experience, and mentorship play critical roles in shaping successful entrepreneurs. The entrepreneurial mindset can be cultivated through continuous learning, self-reflection, and a willingness to step outside one's comfort zone.

The benefits of being an entrepreneur are manifold. One of the most significant advantages is the opportunity to be one's own boss. This autonomy allows entrepreneurs to make decisions that align with their values and vision, creating a work environment that is both fulfilling and motivating. Additionally, entrepreneurship offers the potential for financial rewards. While not guaranteed, the ability to reap the fruits of one's labor and build wealth is a powerful motivator for many entrepreneurs.

Entrepreneurship also provides an avenue for personal growth and development. The challenges and opportunities encountered on the entrepreneurial journey foster a range of skills, including problem-solving, leadership, and strategic thinking. Entrepreneurs often find themselves in situations that require them to learn new things quickly and to adapt to changing circumstances. This constant learning and growth can be incredibly rewarding and can lead to a sense of accomplishment and fulfillment.

However, the entrepreneurial path is not without its challenges. One of the most significant challenges is financial risk. Starting and running a business often requires a substantial financial investment, and there is always the possibility that the venture may not succeed. This financial uncertainty can be stressful and requires careful planning and management. Additionally, entrepreneurs often face long hours and a high level of responsibility. The demands of running a business can take a toll on personal relationships and work-life balance. It is essential for entrepreneurs to find ways to manage stress and to maintain a healthy balance between their professional and personal lives.

Setting entrepreneurial goals is a critical step in the journey. Goals provide direction and focus, helping entrepreneurs to stay motivated and to measure their progress. Effective goal setting involves identifying specific, measurable, achievable, relevant, and time-bound (SMART) goals. This approach ensures that goals are clear and attainable and that there is a plan in place to achieve them. Entrepreneurs should also set both short-term and long-term goals, allowing them to celebrate small victories along the way while keeping their eye on the bigger picture.

An essential aspect of defining entrepreneurship is understanding the various forms it can take. Entrepreneurship is not limited to starting a new business from scratch. It can also involve buying an existing business, franchising, or even intrapreneurship—where individuals innovate and drive change within an existing organization. Each of these paths has its unique characteristics and challenges, and understanding the differences can help aspiring entrepreneurs choose the path that best aligns with their skills, interests, and resources.

Another key element of entrepreneurship is the concept of value creation. Successful entrepreneurs identify unmet needs in the market and develop solutions that create value for customers. This value can take many forms, including convenience, quality, cost savings, or innovation. By focusing on creating value, entrepreneurs can build strong customer relationships and establish a competitive advantage in the market.

The entrepreneurial ecosystem plays a crucial role in supporting entrepreneurs. This ecosystem includes a range of elements such as access to capital, mentorship, education and training programs, and supportive policies and regulations. A strong entrepreneurial ecosystem fosters innovation and growth, providing entrepreneurs with the resources and support they need to succeed. Aspiring entrepreneurs should seek out and leverage these resources to enhance their chances of success.

Networking is another vital component of entrepreneurship. Building a strong network of contacts can provide entrepreneurs with valuable insights, opportunities, and support. Networking can take many forms, from attending industry events and joining professional organizations to leveraging social media and online communities. Effective networking involves building genuine relationships and being open to collaboration and knowledge sharing.

In conclusion, defining entrepreneurship requires a comprehensive understanding of its various dimensions. It is a mindset that embraces creativity, resilience, and a strong sense of purpose. It involves recognizing and acting on opportunities, taking risks, and creating value. While the entrepreneurial journey is filled with challenges and uncertainties, it also offers significant rewards, including autonomy, financial potential, and personal growth. By setting clear goals, understanding the different forms of entrepreneurship, and leveraging the entrepreneurial ecosystem and networks, aspiring entrepreneurs can navigate the complexities of this path and build successful ventures.

Entrepreneurship is also deeply intertwined with the concept of innovation. Innovation is the lifeblood of entrepreneurial ventures, as it allows businesses to differentiate themselves and stay competitive in an ever-evolving market. Entrepreneurs are often seen as innovators who bring new products, services, or business models to the market. This innovative spirit is not limited to technological advancements; it can also include creative approaches to customer service, marketing strategies, and operational efficiencies. Innovation requires a willingness to experiment, take risks, and sometimes fail, but it is through these processes that groundbreaking ideas are born.

The Mindset of a Successful Entrepreneur

The mindset of a successful entrepreneur is a tapestry woven from diverse qualities, each thread contributing to the overall strength and resilience required to navigate the unpredictable landscape of business. At its core, this mindset is characterized by a unique blend of vision, resilience, adaptability, and an unyielding drive for continuous improvement. Understanding and cultivating these attributes can make the difference between merely surviving and truly thriving in the entrepreneurial world.

Vision is the cornerstone of entrepreneurial success. A clear, compelling vision provides direction and purpose, guiding every decision and action. It is the ability to see opportunities where others see obstacles, to envision a future that does not yet exist, and to create a roadmap to bring that vision to life. Successful entrepreneurs are not just dreamers; they are doers. They take their visions and translate them into actionable plans, always keeping their end goals in sight. This vision acts as a North Star, helping them stay focused and motivated, even when faced with significant challenges.

Resilience, another critical component, is the capacity to recover quickly from difficulties. The entrepreneurial journey is fraught with setbacks, failures, and unexpected hurdles. Resilience allows entrepreneurs to bounce back from these challenges, learn from their mistakes, and continue moving forward. It is about maintaining a positive outlook even in the face of adversity and using failures as stepping stones to future success. This quality is often what separates successful entrepreneurs from those who give up when the going gets tough.

Adaptability is equally essential in the ever-changing business environment. Markets evolve, consumer preferences shift, and new competitors emerge. Entrepreneurs must be able to pivot their strategies in response to these changes. This requires a flexible mindset, open to new ideas and willing to experiment. Adaptable entrepreneurs are not afraid to revise their plans or to abandon approaches that are not working. They stay attuned to industry trends and are always ready to seize new opportunities or to mitigate potential threats.

A relentless drive for continuous improvement is also a hallmark of successful entrepreneurs. They are never satisfied with the status quo and are always looking for ways to enhance their products, services, and operations. This drive is fueled by a growth mindset—the belief that abilities and intelligence can be developed through dedication and hard work. Entrepreneurs with a growth mindset see challenges as opportunities to grow, embrace feedback, and are committed to lifelong learning. They invest in their personal and professional development, constantly seeking to expand their knowledge and skills.

Another key aspect of the entrepreneurial mindset is a strong sense of self-discipline. Running a business requires a high level of organization, time management, and the ability to prioritize tasks effectively. Successful entrepreneurs set clear goals and develop structured plans to achieve them. They are disciplined in their work habits, maintaining consistency and focus even when distractions abound. This discipline extends to financial management, ensuring that they manage their resources wisely and make informed decisions.

Risk tolerance is inherent in entrepreneurship. Every business venture involves some degree of risk, whether financial, reputational, or operational. Successful entrepreneurs are comfortable with uncertainty and are willing to take calculated risks to achieve their goals. This does not mean they are reckless; rather, they conduct thorough research and analysis to understand the potential risks and rewards. They are adept at risk management, balancing their bold vision with practical considerations to navigate the complexities of the business landscape effectively.

Effective communication is another vital skill. Entrepreneurs must be able to articulate their vision, inspire their team, and engage with customers, investors, and partners. Strong communication skills help build relationships, foster collaboration, and drive the business forward. This includes not only speaking and writing clearly but also listening actively and empathetically. Understanding the needs and perspectives of stakeholders is crucial for making informed decisions and building a supportive network.

Networking is an invaluable component of the entrepreneurial mindset. Building a strong network of contacts can provide entrepreneurs with valuable insights, opportunities, and support. Networking can take many forms, from attending industry events and joining professional organizations to leveraging social media and online communities. Effective networking involves building genuine relationships and being open to collaboration and knowledge sharing. Entrepreneurs who cultivate robust networks often find themselves with access to resources and advice that can accelerate their business growth.

Passion is the fuel that drives entrepreneurs through the highs and lows of their journey. A deep passion for their work keeps them motivated and committed, even when faced with significant obstacles. This passion is often rooted in a desire to solve a problem, make a difference, or achieve a personal dream. It provides the energy and enthusiasm needed to persevere through tough times and to inspire others to join them in their mission.

Integrity and ethical behavior are foundational to long-term success. Entrepreneurs who build their businesses on a foundation of honesty, transparency, and ethical practices earn the trust and respect of their customers, employees, and partners. This trust is invaluable, fostering loyalty and creating a positive reputation that can set them apart in a competitive market. Ethical entrepreneurs are not only focused on profit but also on making a positive impact on society and conducting their business in a way that aligns with their values.

Lastly, gratitude and humility play a significant role in the entrepreneurial mindset. Successful entrepreneurs recognize the contributions of others and are grateful for the support they receive. They understand that their success is not solely the result of their efforts but also the result of their team, mentors, and supporters. Humility allows them to remain open to feedback, to acknowledge their mistakes, and to continuously strive for improvement. This attitude fosters a positive work environment and encourages continuous learning and growth.

In conclusion, the mindset of a successful entrepreneur is a complex and dynamic blend of vision, resilience, adaptability, continuous improvement, self-discipline, risk tolerance, effective communication, networking, passion, integrity, gratitude, and humility. These attributes create a solid foundation that enables entrepreneurs to navigate the challenges of the business world and to seize opportunities for growth and innovation. By cultivating these qualities, aspiring entrepreneurs can position themselves for success and create ventures that are not only profitable but also impactful and fulfilling. The journey is demanding, but with the right mindset, it is possible to achieve remarkable success and to make a lasting difference.

Entrepreneurs often find that their mindset evolves over time, shaped by their experiences and the lessons they learn along the way. This evolution is a testament to the dynamic nature of entrepreneurship and underscores the importance of being open to change and growth. Reflecting on your journey, celebrating your successes, and understanding your failures are all integral to developing a robust entrepreneurial mindset.

Common Myths About Entrepreneurship

Entrepreneurship is often cloaked in myths that can mislead aspiring business owners. These misconceptions can shape expectations and influence decisions, sometimes to the detriment of those venturing into the entrepreneurial world. Dispelling these myths is essential for anyone aiming to start and grow a successful business.

One prevalent myth is that entrepreneurs are born, not made. This belief suggests that successful entrepreneurs possess innate qualities that cannot be developed. However, research and countless success stories demonstrate that entrepreneurship skills can be learned and honed. While certain personality traits like resilience and creativity may come naturally to some, the vast majority of skills required to run a business—such as financial management, marketing, and strategic planning—can be acquired through education and experience. The journey of entrepreneurship is one of continuous learning and personal growth, accessible to anyone willing to put in the effort.

Another common myth is that you need a groundbreaking idea to start a successful business. Many believe that only revolutionary products or services can lead to entrepreneurial success. While innovation is undoubtedly valuable, many successful businesses are built on improving existing ideas or addressing unmet needs in the market. Entrepreneurs can find success by offering better quality, superior customer service, or more efficient processes than their competitors. The key is to identify a viable market opportunity and execute it well, rather than waiting for a once-in-a-lifetime idea.

The notion that entrepreneurship guarantees immediate wealth is another widespread misconception. Stories of tech moguls and startup founders achieving rapid financial success can create unrealistic expectations. In reality, building a profitable business often takes years of hard work, persistence, and strategic planning. Many entrepreneurs face financial challenges in the early stages, including securing funding, managing cash flow, and sustaining operations. The path to profitability is typically gradual and requires careful management of resources and expenses.

A related myth is that entrepreneurs enjoy total freedom and flexibility. While it is true that being your own boss allows for some degree of control over your schedule, the demands of running a business can be all-consuming. Entrepreneurs often work long hours, especially in the initial phases, handling multiple roles and responsibilities. The pressure to succeed and the need to address various business challenges can limit personal freedom. Effective time management and delegation are crucial to balancing business demands with personal life.

Many people also believe that entrepreneurship is a solitary journey. The image of the lone entrepreneur, toiling away in isolation, is far from accurate. Successful entrepreneurship often involves building a strong network of mentors, advisors, partners, and team members. Collaboration and support from others can provide valuable insights, resources, and emotional encouragement. Entrepreneurs benefit from surrounding themselves with a diverse group of people who bring different skills and perspectives to the table.

The myth that you need significant capital to start a business discourages many potential entrepreneurs. While some ventures do require substantial investment, many successful businesses begin with minimal funding. Bootstrapping, or starting a business with limited resources, is a common approach. Entrepreneurs can leverage personal savings, small loans, or crowdfunding to get started. Additionally, there are numerous cost-effective tools and resources available today that can help entrepreneurs manage and grow their businesses without breaking the bank.

Another misconception is that failure is fatal. The fear of failure can be paralyzing, but it is important to recognize that failure is often a stepping stone to success. Many successful entrepreneurs have experienced multiple failures before achieving their goals. Each setback provides valuable lessons and insights that can be applied to future endeavors. Embracing failure as part of the entrepreneurial process fosters resilience and a willingness to take calculated risks.

The belief that you must be a risk-taker to be an entrepreneur is also misleading. While entrepreneurship does involve risks, successful entrepreneurs are not reckless. They are strategic risk managers who carefully assess potential risks and rewards before making decisions. They conduct thorough research, plan meticulously, and prepare for various scenarios. Risk-taking in entrepreneurship is about being informed and making calculated moves rather than gambling blindly on uncertain outcomes.

A pervasive myth is that once a business is established, the hard work is over. In reality, maintaining and growing a business requires ongoing effort and adaptation. Markets evolve, customer preferences change, and new competitors emerge. Entrepreneurs must continuously innovate, improve their offerings, and stay attuned to market trends. The ability to adapt and pivot in response to changing circumstances is crucial for long-term success.

Many aspiring entrepreneurs also believe that passion alone is enough to ensure success. While passion is a powerful motivator and can drive perseverance, it must be coupled with practical skills and strategic planning. Passion can sustain entrepreneurs through tough times, but it needs to be supported by a solid business model, effective marketing strategies, and sound financial management. Combining passion with pragmatism creates a balanced approach to entrepreneurship.

The myth that you need a formal business plan to start can also be a barrier. While having a business plan is beneficial for setting goals and securing funding, it is not always necessary to begin. Many entrepreneurs start with a simple concept and refine their business model as they go. The key is to remain flexible and open to adjusting the plan based on real-world feedback and experiences. The initial focus should be on validating the idea and establishing a market presence.

Lastly, there is a misconception that entrepreneurship is only for the young and tech-savvy. While the media often highlights young tech entrepreneurs, people of all ages and backgrounds can succeed in entrepreneurship. Experience, industry knowledge, and a strong network can be powerful assets. Older entrepreneurs bring valuable skills and insights gained from their careers, and they often have a clearer understanding of their strengths and weaknesses. Age and background should not be seen as barriers but rather as unique advantages that can contribute to entrepreneurial success.

In summary, understanding and debunking common myths about entrepreneurship is crucial for aspiring business owners. Entrepreneurship is not reserved for a select few with innate talents or groundbreaking ideas. It is a journey of learning, persistence, and strategic risk management. Success requires more than passion; it demands a combination of practical skills, resilience, and the ability to adapt to changing circumstances. By dispelling these myths, potential entrepreneurs can approach their ventures with realistic expectations and a better chance of achieving their goals.

Breaking free from these myths allows aspiring entrepreneurs to navigate the challenges of starting and growing a business with a clear and informed mindset. Embracing a realistic perspective helps in setting achievable goals and developing strategies that align with the true nature of entrepreneurship.

Benefits and Challenges of Being an Entrepreneur

Entrepreneurship is a journey filled with both rewards and hurdles. Understanding the benefits and challenges of being an entrepreneur can help aspiring business owners prepare for what lies ahead and navigate the intricate path of starting and managing a business.

One of the most significant benefits of being an entrepreneur is the opportunity to pursue your passions. Many people dream of turning their interests and hobbies into a livelihood, and entrepreneurship provides a platform to do just that. When you work on something you are passionate about, it doesn't feel like work. This intrinsic motivation can drive you to overcome obstacles and maintain your enthusiasm even during tough times.

Another advantage is the autonomy and control that come with running your own business. As an entrepreneur, you are the decision-maker. You have the freedom to shape your business according to your vision and values. This autonomy allows you to experiment with new ideas, pivot strategies, and create a work environment that aligns with your personal and professional goals. The sense of ownership and responsibility can be incredibly empowering.

Financial potential is another appealing aspect of entrepreneurship. While it often takes time to see significant financial returns, the possibility of unlimited income is a powerful incentive. Unlike a salaried job, where your earnings are capped, entrepreneurship allows you to reap the benefits of your hard work and innovation. Successful entrepreneurs often experience financial growth that outpaces traditional career paths, leading to long-term wealth and financial independence.

Entrepreneurship also fosters personal growth and development. The challenges and responsibilities of running a business require you to develop a wide range of skills, from leadership and time management to problem-solving and strategic thinking. This continuous learning process can be immensely rewarding, as you build confidence and resilience. Moreover, overcoming the inevitable setbacks and failures teaches valuable lessons that contribute to personal and professional maturity.

The ability to make a positive impact is another compelling reason to become an entrepreneur. Many entrepreneurs are driven by the desire to solve problems, create value, and contribute to their communities. Whether it's through innovative products, exceptional services, or social enterprises, entrepreneurs have the power to influence and improve the world around them. This sense of purpose and contribution can be deeply fulfilling.

However, the entrepreneurial journey is not without its challenges. One of the most daunting aspects is the financial risk involved. Starting a business often requires significant investment, and there is always the possibility that the venture might not succeed. Entrepreneurs must be prepared to face financial uncertainty and manage cash flow effectively. This may involve securing funding, budgeting meticulously, and being prepared for lean periods.

The workload and stress associated with entrepreneurship can also be overwhelming. Unlike traditional employment, where responsibilities are often clearly defined and limited, entrepreneurs must wear many hats. From managing operations and finances to marketing and customer service, the demands can be relentless. The pressure to succeed and the responsibility for the business's success or failure can lead to high levels of stress and burnout.

Balancing work and personal life is another significant challenge for entrepreneurs. The dedication and time required to build a business can encroach on personal time, affecting relationships and overall well-being. Entrepreneurs must develop effective time management strategies and set boundaries to ensure they maintain a healthy work-life balance. Delegating tasks and building a reliable team can also help alleviate some of the pressure.

Another challenge is the constant need for adaptability and resilience. The business landscape is dynamic, with market conditions, consumer preferences, and technological advancements continuously evolving. Entrepreneurs must be able to pivot and adapt their strategies to stay relevant and competitive. This requires a proactive mindset, the ability to embrace change, and the resilience to bounce back from setbacks.

Entrepreneurship can also be a lonely journey. The responsibility of making critical decisions and the intensity of the workload can isolate entrepreneurs from their social circles. Building a support network of mentors, advisors, and fellow entrepreneurs is crucial. These connections provide valuable advice, emotional support, and a sense of community. Networking and seeking out entrepreneurial groups or forums can help mitigate feelings of isolation.

Navigating regulatory and legal requirements is another challenge that entrepreneurs must face. Understanding and complying with laws related to business operations, taxation, employment, and intellectual property can be complex and time-consuming. Entrepreneurs need to stay informed about relevant regulations and seek professional legal and financial advice to ensure compliance and avoid potential pitfalls.

Despite these challenges, the entrepreneurial journey offers unparalleled opportunities for innovation and creativity. Entrepreneurs have the freedom to experiment with new ideas, challenge the status quo, and bring novel solutions to market. This creative freedom can lead to groundbreaking products and services that make a significant impact. The satisfaction of seeing your ideas come to life and succeed in the market is a unique reward of entrepreneurship.

Moreover, entrepreneurship allows for the building of a legacy. Many entrepreneurs are motivated by the desire to create something enduring that outlives them. A successful business can become a lasting legacy, providing opportunities for future generations and contributing to the economy and society. The ability to shape and leave behind a meaningful legacy is a powerful motivator for many business owners.

In conclusion, being an entrepreneur comes with a blend of benefits and challenges. The freedom to pursue your passions, the potential for financial growth, and the opportunity to make a positive impact are among the key advantages. However, financial risk, workload, stress, and the need for adaptability are significant hurdles that require careful management. By understanding these aspects, aspiring entrepreneurs can prepare themselves for the realities of the entrepreneurial journey and increase their chances of success. Embracing both the rewards and the challenges allows for a balanced and informed approach to entrepreneurship, ultimately leading to personal fulfillment and professional achievement.

Recognizing the dual nature of entrepreneurship—the highs of success and the lows of potential setbacks—can also help in developing a more resilient and prepared mindset. Entrepreneurs who are aware of the potential challenges can proactively seek solutions and strategies to mitigate risks and enhance their chances of success.

Setting Your Entrepreneurial Goals

Setting clear and achievable entrepreneurial goals is a pivotal step in the journey of starting and growing a successful business. Goals provide direction, motivation, and a benchmark for measuring progress. They help entrepreneurs stay focused on what truly matters and navigate the myriad of challenges that arise. Crafting these goals involves a blend of vision, strategy, and practicality, ensuring they are both inspiring and attainable.

Begin with your long-term vision. This is the overarching picture of what you want your business to become. It encapsulates your aspirations, values, and the impact you wish to make. For instance, an entrepreneur starting a sustainable fashion brand might envision creating a global movement that redefines the industry standards for eco-friendly practices. This vision serves as the North Star, guiding every decision and action you take.

Once you have a clear vision, break it down into more manageable, medium-term objectives. These are milestones that bridge the gap between your current position and your long-term vision. They should be specific and time-bound, providing a clear roadmap. For example, if your vision is to become a leader in sustainable fashion, a medium-term goal could be to launch a fully sustainable product line within the next two years. This goal gives you something concrete to strive for and a timeframe to work within.

Short-term goals are the actionable steps you need to take to achieve your medium-term objectives. These should be even more specific and have a shorter timeframe, such as six months to a year. Continuing with the sustainable fashion example, a short-term goal might be to source eco-friendly materials and secure partnerships with sustainable suppliers within the next six months. These goals are the building blocks of your larger vision, providing immediate tasks that drive progress.

To ensure your goals are effective, they should adhere to the SMART criteria: Specific, Measurable, Achievable, Relevant, and Time-bound. Specific goals clearly define what needs to be accomplished. Measurable goals allow you to track progress and determine when they have been achieved. Achievable goals are realistic and attainable given your resources and constraints. Relevant goals align with your broader vision and business objectives. Time-bound goals have a clear deadline, creating a sense of urgency and focus.

Setting goals is not a one-time task but an ongoing process that requires regular review and adjustment. The business environment is dynamic, and as you progress, you may encounter new opportunities and challenges that necessitate a shift in your goals. Regularly reviewing your goals ensures they remain aligned with your vision and current circumstances. This iterative process allows you to stay agile and responsive to changes.

A crucial aspect of achieving your goals is breaking them down into actionable steps. Large goals can often feel overwhelming, but by dividing them into smaller tasks, they become more manageable and less daunting. For example, if your goal is to launch a new product, break it down into steps such as market research, product design, prototyping, testing, and marketing. Each step should have its own mini-goals and timeline, creating a clear path to follow.

Accountability is another key factor in goal achievement. Sharing your goals with a mentor, business partner, or even a friend can create a sense of responsibility and encouragement. Regularly updating them on your progress and challenges can provide motivation and support. Additionally, consider establishing regular check-ins with yourself or your team to assess progress, celebrate achievements, and address any obstacles.

Visualization is a powerful tool in goal setting. Taking the time to vividly imagine the successful achievement of your goals can boost motivation and clarify the steps needed to get there. Visualization techniques can include creating vision boards, writing detailed descriptions of your future success, or simply taking a few minutes each day to mentally picture your accomplishments. This practice can enhance focus and determination.

While it's important to set ambitious goals, it's equally crucial to remain flexible. The entrepreneurial journey is unpredictable, and rigidly sticking to a plan in the face of new information or changing circumstances can be detrimental. Being open to revising your goals as needed, without losing sight of your overall vision, allows you to adapt and thrive in a dynamic environment.

Celebrating small wins along the way is vital for maintaining motivation and morale. Each step forward, no matter how small, is progress and deserves recognition. Celebrations can be as simple as acknowledging your achievements with your team, taking a moment to reflect on your progress, or rewarding yourself with a small treat. These moments of celebration can rejuvenate your energy and reinforce your commitment to your goals.

Setting entrepreneurial goals also involves understanding and mitigating risks. Every goal carries inherent risks, and being prepared to address them can make the difference between success and failure. Conducting a thorough risk assessment for each goal, identifying potential obstacles, and developing contingency plans can help you navigate challenges more effectively. This proactive approach builds resilience and confidence.

Engaging with your team in the goal-setting process can foster a sense of ownership and alignment. When team members contribute to defining goals, they are more likely to be committed to achieving them.

Collaborative goal setting encourages diverse perspectives, enhances creativity, and builds a unified effort towards common objectives. Regular communication and feedback loops ensure everyone stays aligned and motivated.

Finally, maintaining a positive mindset is crucial throughout the goal-setting and achievement process. Entrepreneurship is fraught with ups and downs, and a positive attitude can help you stay focused and resilient. Embrace challenges as opportunities for growth, learn from setbacks, and maintain a forward-looking perspective. A positive mindset not only enhances your personal well-being but also inspires and motivates those around you.

In summary, setting entrepreneurial goals is a multifaceted process that involves envisioning your long-term aspirations, breaking them down into manageable steps, and continuously adapting to changes. By adhering to the SMART criteria, breaking down goals into actionable steps, ensuring accountability, and maintaining flexibility, entrepreneurs can navigate the complexities of their journey. Celebrating small wins, engaging with your team, and maintaining a positive mindset further enhance the likelihood of achieving your goals. Through careful planning, continuous learning, and unwavering determination, you can turn your entrepreneurial vision into reality and build a successful, impactful business.

The entrepreneurial journey is not just about reaching the destination but also about the experiences and growth you encounter along the way. Setting clear and well-structured goals ensures that you stay on course, even when faced with the inevitable challenges of running a business. It's important to remember that goals are not static; they evolve as you and your business grow. This flexibility allows you to pivot when necessary and seize new opportunities that align with your overarching vision.

Chapter 2

Identifying Business Opportunities

Understanding Market Needs

Understanding market needs is the cornerstone of building a successful business. Without a deep grasp of what your potential customers want, need, and value, even the best ideas can fall flat. This process begins with market research, which involves gathering, analyzing, and interpreting information about a market, including the products or services that will be offered, the target audience, and the competition. It's a pivotal step that informs strategy, product development, marketing, and sales.

Imagine you have an idea for a new product. Maybe it's a tech gadget that you believe will revolutionize the way people manage their daily tasks. Before you invest time and resources into developing this product, you need to ensure there is a demand for it. This is where market research comes into play. Start by identifying your target market. Who are the potential buyers of your product? Consider demographics such as age, gender, income level, education, and geographic location. Psychographics, which include values, interests, lifestyles, and behaviors, are equally important. Understanding these factors helps you tailor your product and marketing efforts to meet the specific needs and preferences of your target audience.

Once you have a clear picture of your target market, engage directly with potential customers to gather insights. Surveys, interviews, and focus groups are effective tools for this purpose. Surveys allow you to reach a broad audience quickly, while interviews and focus groups provide more in-depth qualitative data. Ask questions that uncover pain points, desires, and expectations. For instance, you could ask, "What challenges do you face with your current productivity tools?" or "What features would make a new tech gadget indispensable for you?" These responses will provide valuable insights into what your market needs and how your product can address those needs.

Analyzing existing data is another crucial aspect of understanding market needs. Look at industry reports, sales data, and consumer trends to identify patterns and opportunities. For example, if you notice a growing trend in remote work, this could influence the features and design of your tech gadget to cater to remote workers' specific requirements. Competitor analysis is also vital. Study your competitors' products, marketing strategies, and customer feedback. What are they doing well? Where are they falling short? This information helps you identify gaps in the market that your product can fill.

Social media platforms are a goldmine for understanding market needs. People freely express their opinions, frustrations, and desires online. Monitoring social media conversations related to your industry or product category can provide real-time insights. Tools like social listening software can help you track mentions, sentiment, and trends. By engaging with users directly, you can ask follow-up questions and gain deeper insights into their needs and preferences.

In addition to direct engagement and data analysis, observational research can reveal unarticulated needs. This involves observing how potential customers interact with products in real-world settings. For example, if you are developing a new kitchen gadget, watch how people use their current tools while cooking. What difficulties do they encounter? What workarounds do they use? These observations can lead to innovative solutions that directly address user pain points.

Once you have gathered and analyzed your data, the next step is to synthesize it into actionable insights. Create detailed customer personas that represent different segments of your target market. Each persona should include demographic and psychographic information, as well as specific needs, pain points, and preferences. For example, one persona might be "Tech-Savvy Tom," a 30-year-old remote worker who values efficiency and integrates the latest technology into his daily routine. Another might be "Busy Brenda," a 45-year-old working mother who needs simple, reliable tools to manage her household and work responsibilities. These personas help you visualize your customers and keep their needs at the forefront of your product development and marketing efforts.

With a clear understanding of your market needs, you can now develop a value proposition that articulates how your product meets those needs better than any existing alternatives. This value proposition should be the foundation of your marketing and sales strategies. For instance, if your tech gadget offers unique features that simplify remote work, your value proposition might be, "Revolutionize your remote work experience with our innovative, all-in-one productivity tool designed for efficiency and ease."

Testing your assumptions is a critical step before fully launching your product. Create prototypes or minimum viable products (MVPs) and get them into the hands of your target customers. Collect feedback and observe how they interact with your product. Does it solve their pain points? Are there any unforeseen issues? Use this feedback to refine your product until it truly meets the market needs.

After launching your product, continue to monitor market needs and gather feedback. The market is dynamic, and customer needs can evolve over time. Stay engaged with your customers through surveys, social media, and direct interactions. Regularly review sales data, customer reviews, and market trends. This ongoing process ensures that your product remains relevant and continues to meet the changing needs of your market.

Storytelling can be a powerful tool in understanding and communicating market needs. Share stories of how your product has made a difference in real customers' lives. These stories not only build credibility and emotional connection but also provide insights into how your product is being used and the value it provides. For instance, a testimonial from a customer who improved their productivity dramatically by using your tech gadget can highlight features that resonate most with your audience.

Understanding market needs also involves recognizing and addressing barriers to adoption. Even if your product meets a significant need, there may be obstacles that prevent customers from purchasing or using it. These barriers could be related to price, perceived complexity, or trust. Conducting thorough research to identify these barriers allows you to develop strategies to overcome them. For example, offering a free trial or a money-back guarantee can reduce the perceived risk and encourage potential customers to try your product.

Building a community around your product can further enhance your understanding of market needs. Create forums, social media groups, or user communities where customers can share their experiences, ask questions, and provide feedback. These communities not only foster customer loyalty but also serve as a continuous source of insights. Engaging with your community allows you to stay attuned to their evolving needs and preferences.

Understanding market needs is an ongoing, iterative process that requires active engagement, thorough research, and a willingness to adapt. By deeply understanding your target market, you can develop products and services that truly resonate with customers and stand out in a competitive landscape. This customer-centric approach not only drives initial success but also ensures long-term growth and sustainability. Through careful observation, direct engagement, and continuous feedback, you can create value that meets and exceeds market expectations, ultimately building a loyal customer base and a thriving business.

Consistency in addressing market needs is paramount. As your business grows, the scale of your operations and the diversity of your customer base will expand, presenting new challenges and opportunities. It's essential to maintain the agility and responsiveness that characterized your early stages. A robust customer feedback system should be institutionalized, allowing you to capture insights across various touchpoints, such as customer service interactions, product reviews, and direct responses to marketing campaigns.

Evaluating Business Ideas

When evaluating business ideas, the excitement of innovation can often overshadow the practical considerations necessary for success. It's crucial to methodically assess each idea's potential to ensure it aligns with market needs, is financially viable, and sustainable in the long term. This process involves several steps, each designed to provide a clear picture of the idea's strengths and weaknesses.

The first step in evaluating a business idea is to understand the problem it aims to solve. Every successful business addresses a specific need or pain point. Start by clearly defining the problem your idea intends to tackle. For instance, if your idea is a new type of eco-friendly packaging, identify the environmental issues caused by traditional packaging and how your solution mitigates these problems. This clarity helps in articulating the value proposition of your idea.

Next, validate the market demand. Conduct thorough market research to gauge the interest and need for your product or service. Surveys, focus groups, and interviews with potential customers can provide valuable insights. For example, if you're considering launching a meal delivery service, you might survey busy professionals to understand their dining habits and preferences. Look for patterns that indicate a genuine demand for your solution. Additionally, analyzing industry reports and market trends can offer a broader perspective on the potential market size and growth prospects.

Competitive analysis is another critical component. Identifying and understanding your competitors helps you determine your unique selling proposition (USP). Examine what they offer, their pricing strategies, strengths, and weaknesses. For instance, if you're developing a new fitness app, review existing apps to see what features are popular and where they fall short. Your USP might be a unique feature or a better user experience that sets your app apart. This analysis also helps you avoid overcrowded markets where differentiation might be challenging.

Financial feasibility is a fundamental aspect of evaluating a business idea. Develop a detailed financial plan that includes initial investment, operating costs, revenue projections, and break-even analysis. Calculate how much capital you need to start and sustain the business until it becomes profitable. For example, if your idea is to open a boutique coffee shop, factor in costs like rent, equipment, supplies, salaries, and marketing. Estimate your monthly revenue based on realistic customer traffic and average spend per visit. This financial scrutiny ensures you have a clear understanding of the economic realities and helps in securing funding from investors or lenders.

Assessing the scalability of your idea is vital for long-term success. Consider whether the business can grow and how easily it can adapt to increased demand. For instance, a software-based business might scale more easily than a brick-and-mortar store, which has physical limitations. Think about the resources, processes, and systems required to expand your business. Can your supply chain handle larger volumes? Do you have the infrastructure to support growth? Scalability ensures that your business can evolve and thrive as it gains traction.

Evaluate the risks associated with your business idea. Every venture comes with uncertainties, and identifying potential risks helps in developing mitigation strategies. These risks can be market-related, financial, operational, or regulatory. For example, launching a new healthcare product might involve regulatory hurdles, while a tech startup might face rapid technological changes. Conduct a SWOT analysis (Strengths, Weaknesses, Opportunities, Threats) to systematically examine these factors. Understanding risks allows you to plan proactively and build resilience.

The team behind the idea plays a crucial role in its success. Assess whether you have the right skills and expertise to execute the business plan. If not, consider bringing in co-founders or hiring employees with the necessary experience. For example, if your idea involves developing a complex mobile app, having a skilled software developer on your team is essential. A strong, complementary team increases the chances of successfully bringing your idea to life and navigating challenges along the way.

Customer feedback can provide invaluable insights during the evaluation process. Create a prototype or a minimum viable product (MVP) and test it with a small group of potential customers. Their feedback can highlight strengths, identify shortcomings, and suggest improvements. For instance, if you're developing a new kitchen gadget, having home cooks test it in real kitchen scenarios can uncover practical issues that you might not have anticipated. This iterative process ensures that your final product is well-tuned to meet customer needs.

Consider the timing of your business idea. Market conditions, economic cycles, and seasonal trends can significantly impact your business's success.

Launching an idea too early or too late can affect its reception. For instance, a travel-related business might face challenges during economic downturns or global travel restrictions. Stay informed about industry trends and economic forecasts to choose the optimal time for your launch.

Legal and regulatory considerations are also crucial. Ensure that your business idea complies with all relevant laws and regulations. This includes intellectual property rights, business licenses, zoning laws, and industry-specific regulations. For instance, if you're starting a food business, you need to comply with health and safety regulations. Consulting with legal experts can help you navigate these complexities and avoid potential legal issues down the road.

Finally, align your business idea with your personal goals and values. Consider whether it fits your long-term vision, passion, and lifestyle. Building a business requires significant time, energy, and commitment. If your idea resonates with your personal aspirations, you're more likely to stay motivated and overcome obstacles. For example, if you're passionate about sustainability, a business that promotes eco-friendly products will be more fulfilling and align with your values.

To illustrate, let's consider the case of Spanx, the highly successful shapewear company founded by Sara Blakely. Blakely identified a clear problem: women wanted comfortable, effective undergarments that smoothed their figures. She validated market demand by talking to potential customers and realized that existing products didn't meet their needs. By creating a unique, high-quality product, she differentiated Spanx from competitors. Blakely meticulously planned the financial aspects, starting with a small budget and reinvesting profits to grow the business. She also leveraged customer feedback to continuously improve her products. Her personal passion for empowering women and her innovative approach to problem-solving drove Spanx to become a market leader.

Evaluating business ideas involves a comprehensive and systematic approach. By thoroughly understanding the problem, validating market demand, analyzing competitors, ensuring financial feasibility, assessing scalability, identifying risks, building the right team, gathering customer feedback, considering timing, addressing legal concerns, and aligning with personal goals, you can significantly increase the chances of success. This rigorous evaluation process not only helps in selecting the most promising ideas but also lays a solid foundation for building a sustainable and thriving business. Each step is a critical piece of the puzzle, contributing to a well-rounded and robust business strategy that can withstand challenges and capitalize on opportunities.

By adhering to this structured approach, entrepreneurs can transform raw ideas into viable business ventures. However, the journey from concept to execution is often complex and filled with unforeseen challenges. It's essential to remain adaptable and open to revisiting and refining your evaluations as new information and insights emerge.

Conducting Feasibility Studies

Before launching any business venture, conducting a feasibility study is crucial. This process assesses the viability of a business idea, ensuring it can thrive in the competitive market. A comprehensive feasibility study involves evaluating various aspects of the proposed business, including market potential, financial requirements, operational logistics, and legal considerations. This chapter delves into the essential components of a feasibility study and offers practical steps to execute one effectively.

The first step in conducting a feasibility study is to understand the market landscape. This involves identifying the target market, analyzing customer needs, and assessing the competitive environment. Start by defining your target customers, considering demographics such as age, gender, income level, and geographic location. Understanding who your customers are helps tailor your products or services to meet their specific needs.

Next, gather data on market demand. This can be done through surveys, interviews, focus groups, and market research reports. For instance, if you plan to open a new café, survey local residents to understand their coffee consumption habits and preferences. Analyzing this data provides insights into potential demand and helps predict sales volume.

Competitive analysis is another critical component. Identify your direct and indirect competitors and evaluate their strengths and weaknesses. Visit their locations, if applicable, and observe their operations. Analyze their pricing strategies, customer service, product offerings, and marketing techniques. This information helps you identify gaps in the market and opportunities for differentiation. For example, if competitors lack a cozy ambiance or offer limited menu options, your café could focus on creating a unique atmosphere and offering a diverse menu to attract customers.

Financial feasibility is fundamental to any feasibility study. Prepare a detailed financial plan that includes startup costs, operating expenses, revenue projections, and break-even analysis. Startup costs encompass everything needed to launch the business, such as equipment, inventory, permits, and marketing expenses. Operating expenses include ongoing costs like rent, utilities, salaries, and supplies. Revenue projections estimate how much money the business will generate, based on market demand and pricing strategies. Break-even analysis determines how long it will take for the business to become profitable.

For instance, if you're planning to launch an online clothing store, calculate the costs of purchasing inventory, building a website, and marketing your products. Estimate monthly expenses such as website maintenance, shipping costs, and advertising. Project your revenue based on expected sales volume and average order value. This financial scrutiny ensures you have a clear understanding of the economic realities and helps in securing funding from investors or lenders.

Operational logistics are another crucial aspect of a feasibility study. Assess the resources, processes, and systems required to operate the business efficiently.

This includes supply chain management, production processes, distribution channels, and customer service strategies. For example, if your business involves manufacturing a product, evaluate your suppliers' reliability, production capacity, and lead times. Ensure you have a robust distribution network to deliver products to customers promptly. Develop efficient customer service processes to handle inquiries, complaints, and returns.

Legal and regulatory considerations must also be addressed. Ensure your business complies with all relevant laws and regulations, including zoning laws, licensing requirements, health and safety standards, and industry-specific regulations. For instance, if you're opening a restaurant, you need to comply with health codes, obtain a food service license, and ensure your premises meet fire safety regulations. Consulting with legal experts can help you navigate these complexities and avoid potential legal issues down the road.

Assessing the risks associated with the business is an essential part of a feasibility study. Identify potential risks and develop strategies to mitigate them. These risks can be market-related, financial, operational, or regulatory. For example, launching a new technology product might involve risks related to rapid technological changes, intellectual property issues, or market acceptance. Conduct a SWOT analysis (Strengths, Weaknesses, Opportunities, Threats) to systematically examine these factors. Understanding risks allows you to plan proactively and build resilience.

Another critical component is evaluating the management team's capabilities. The success of any business heavily relies on the skills and experience of its leaders. Assess whether you have the right skills and expertise to execute the business plan. If not, consider bringing in co-founders or hiring employees with the necessary experience. For instance, if your business idea involves developing a complex software application, having a skilled software developer on your team is essential. A strong, complementary team increases the chances of successfully bringing your idea to life and navigating challenges along the way.

Customer feedback plays a crucial role during the feasibility study. Create a prototype or a minimum viable product (MVP) and test it with a small group of potential customers. Their feedback can highlight strengths, identify shortcomings, and suggest improvements. For instance, if you're developing a new kitchen gadget, having home cooks test it in real kitchen scenarios can uncover practical issues that you might not have anticipated. This iterative process ensures that your final product is well-tuned to meet customer needs.

Consider the timing of your business idea. Market conditions, economic cycles, and seasonal trends can significantly impact your business's success. Launching an idea too early or too late can affect its reception. For instance, a travel-related business might face challenges during economic downturns or global travel restrictions. Stay informed about industry trends and economic forecasts to choose the optimal time for your launch.

Sustainability and social responsibility are increasingly important to consumers and can influence the success of your business. Evaluate how your business practices impact the environment and society, and consider implementing sustainable practices and corporate social responsibility (CSR) initiatives. For example, a fashion brand could use eco-friendly materials and ethical manufacturing processes, while a tech company might invest in renewable energy and community programs. These efforts not only contribute to a positive brand image but also resonate with consumers who prioritize ethical consumption.

Networking and building relationships with industry peers, mentors, and potential investors can provide valuable support and insights. Engage with industry associations, attend conferences, and participate in networking events to expand your professional network. These connections can offer guidance, open doors to new opportunities, and provide access to resources that can help you navigate the challenges of starting and growing a business. For instance, a mentor with experience in your industry can provide strategic advice and help you avoid common pitfalls, while investors can offer financial backing and valuable industry connections.

In conclusion, a feasibility study is a comprehensive and systematic approach to evaluating a business idea's potential for success. By thoroughly researching the market, analyzing competitors, ensuring financial viability, assessing operational logistics, addressing legal and regulatory requirements, evaluating risks, and gathering customer feedback, you can make informed decisions about whether to proceed with your business idea. This rigorous evaluation process not only helps in selecting the most promising ideas but also lays a solid foundation for building a sustainable and thriving business.

A well-conducted feasibility study provides a roadmap, guiding entrepreneurs through the intricate process of transforming an idea into a profitable venture. Armed with detailed insights and data, you can anticipate challenges, capitalize on strengths, and strategically plan your next steps. This forward-thinking approach significantly increases the likelihood of success and minimizes the risk of costly mistakes.

Identifying Niche Markets

Discovering a niche market can be the key to standing out in a crowded business landscape. Identifying a niche involves pinpointing specific, underserved segments within a broader market, and creating products or services that cater to these unique needs. The journey to finding your niche begins with understanding the broader market landscape and then narrowing down to a more focused group of potential customers who have distinct preferences, challenges, and demands.

To start, immerse yourself in market research. This involves gathering data about the broader industry, identifying trends, and understanding customer behavior. Utilize tools like surveys, focus groups, and online research to gather insights. Pay attention to emerging trends and shifts in consumer preferences. For example, the rise of eco-conscious consumers has created numerous niche markets in sustainable products and services. In-depth research helps you uncover these opportunities and understand the specific needs of potential niche markets.

Next, analyze your competitors. Identify businesses that operate within the broader market and observe which customer segments they serve. Look for gaps in their offerings or areas where customer needs are not fully met. This competitive analysis helps you spot opportunities for differentiation. For instance, if competitors in the fitness industry primarily target young adults, there might be an untapped market for fitness programs tailored to older adults or those with specific health conditions.

Engage with potential customers directly to gain deeper insights. Conduct interviews or participate in online forums and social media groups where your potential customers are active. Listen to their discussions, challenges, and desires. This qualitative data is invaluable for understanding the nuances of your niche market. For example, engaging with a community of hobbyist bakers could reveal a demand for specialized baking tools or unique ingredient kits that are not widely available.

Leverage your personal interests and expertise. Often, the best niche markets align with your passions and skills. Reflect on your hobbies, professional background, and areas of interest. Your unique perspective can help identify niche opportunities that others might overlook. For instance, if you have a background in pet care and a passion for technology, you might identify a niche market for smart pet care devices.

Develop a clear value proposition for your niche market. This involves articulating how your product or service addresses the specific needs and pain points of your niche audience. A compelling value proposition differentiates you from competitors and resonates with your target customers. For example, a skincare brand focusing on sensitive skin could highlight its use of hypoallergenic ingredients and rigorous testing processes to ensure safety and efficacy.

Once you have identified a potential niche market, validate your idea by testing it with a small group of target customers. This could involve creating a prototype, offering a limited product launch, or conducting a pilot program. Gather feedback and refine your offering based on real-world responses. This iterative process helps ensure that your product or service truly meets the needs of your niche market and reduces the risk of launching a product that fails to gain traction.

Consider the scalability of your niche market. While niche markets are inherently smaller than broader markets, they should still offer sufficient growth potential. Evaluate the size of your target audience, their purchasing power, and the potential for market expansion. For example, a niche market for gluten-free snacks initially targeting a local community could have broader appeal as awareness and demand for gluten-free products grow globally.

Marketing to a niche audience requires targeted strategies. Develop a marketing plan that focuses on the specific channels and messages that resonate with your niche market. Utilize social media platforms, online communities, and content marketing to reach your audience effectively. For instance, a niche brand specializing in organic baby products might create educational content about the benefits of organic materials and share it through parenting blogs, forums, and social media groups.

Building strong relationships with your niche customers is crucial for long-term success. Engage with your audience regularly, solicit their feedback, and involve them in the development process. Creating a loyal community around your brand can lead to word-of-mouth referrals and organic growth. For example, a niche coffee brand could host events, offer exclusive memberships, and create a platform for coffee enthusiasts to share their experiences and preferences.

Stay adaptable and open to evolving your niche. Market dynamics and customer preferences can change over time, and being flexible allows you to stay relevant. Continuously monitor industry trends, customer feedback, and competitive activities. This proactive approach helps you identify new opportunities within your niche and adapt your offerings accordingly. For instance, a niche apparel brand might expand its product line to include sustainable fabrics as consumer demand for eco-friendly fashion grows.

Leveraging technology can enhance your ability to serve your niche market effectively. Utilize data analytics to gain deeper insights into customer behavior and preferences. Implement customer relationship management (CRM) systems to personalize interactions and improve customer service. For example, an online store targeting a niche market for vintage collectibles could use data analytics to recommend items based on past purchases and browsing history, enhancing the shopping experience.

Consider collaborations and partnerships to strengthen your presence in the niche market. Partnering with influencers, complementary brands, or industry experts can amplify your reach and credibility. For instance, a niche health supplement brand could collaborate with fitness influencers to promote its products and reach a broader audience within the fitness community.

Finally, ensure that your niche market aligns with your long-term business goals and values. While niche markets can offer lucrative opportunities, they should also be a good fit for your business vision and mission. Reflect on how serving this niche market contributes to your overall business objectives and whether it aligns with your core values. For example, a niche brand committed to sustainability should ensure that all aspects of its operations, from sourcing to packaging, reflect its commitment to environmental responsibility.

In conclusion, identifying a niche market involves thorough research, understanding customer needs, analyzing competitors, and leveraging personal

interests and expertise. A successful niche strategy
requires a clear value proposition, targeted marketing,
and strong customer relationships. By staying
adaptable and leveraging technology, you can
effectively serve your niche market and achieve long-
term success. With careful planning and execution,
discovering and cultivating a niche market can
transform a business idea into a thriving venture,
offering unique solutions that resonate deeply with a
specific audience.

Using SWOT Analysis to Assess Opportunities

SWOT analysis is a strategic planning tool used to
understand the internal and external factors that can
impact an organization's success. By examining
strengths, weaknesses, opportunities, and threats,
businesses can develop strategies to exploit
opportunities and mitigate risks. To effectively use
SWOT analysis, it's essential to understand each
component and how they interrelate.

Begin by identifying internal strengths. These are the
positive attributes and resources within the
organization. Strengths can include a strong brand
reputation, loyal customer base, unique technology,
efficient processes, and skilled workforce. For
example, a company known for its innovative
products can leverage its strong research and
development team to stay ahead of competitors.
Understanding these strengths allows the
organization to capitalize on what it does best.

Next, assess internal weaknesses. These are areas where the organization may be lacking or facing challenges. Weaknesses can include outdated technology, limited resources, poor location, or gaps in skills among employees. Recognizing weaknesses is crucial because it highlights areas that need improvement. For instance, a company with a weak online presence in an increasingly digital market must address this gap to remain competitive. A candid assessment of weaknesses enables the organization to develop strategies to overcome or minimize these shortcomings.

After evaluating internal factors, consider external opportunities. Opportunities are favorable external conditions that the organization can exploit to its advantage. These can arise from market trends, technological advancements, regulatory changes, or shifts in consumer behavior. For example, the growing demand for sustainable products presents an opportunity for businesses to develop eco-friendly alternatives. Identifying opportunities requires staying informed about industry trends, customer needs, and emerging markets. By aligning strengths with opportunities, organizations can create value and gain a competitive edge.

It's equally important to identify external threats. Threats are external factors that could harm the organization. These can include economic downturns, increased competition, changing regulations, or negative press. For instance, a new competitor entering the market with a disruptive technology poses a significant threat. Recognizing threats enables the organization to develop contingency plans and proactive measures to protect its interests. By understanding potential threats, businesses can mitigate risks and avoid pitfalls.

Once all components are identified, it's time to analyze how they interact. This involves looking at how strengths can be used to maximize opportunities and minimize threats. For example, a company with a robust distribution network (strength) can quickly capitalize on a growing market demand (opportunity) while also preparing to counter new competitors (threat). Conversely, consider how weaknesses might hinder the ability to exploit opportunities or exacerbate threats. A business with a slow product development cycle (weakness) might struggle to keep up with rapidly changing consumer preferences (threat).

To illustrate the power of SWOT analysis, consider a hypothetical small business: a local bakery. The bakery's strengths might include high-quality, artisanal products and a loyal customer base. Its weaknesses could be limited marketing reach and a small physical space. Opportunities might involve the increasing trend of online food delivery and a growing interest in locally sourced ingredients. Threats could include the opening of new bakeries in the area and rising ingredient costs.

By conducting a SWOT analysis, the bakery can develop a strategic plan. It could leverage its strengths by promoting its artisanal quality and local ingredients through an enhanced online presence and delivery service. Addressing weaknesses might involve investing in digital marketing and expanding the physical space to accommodate more customers. To capitalize on opportunities, the bakery could partner with local farms for ingredients and offer unique, seasonal products. To mitigate threats, it could implement cost-saving measures and create loyalty programs to retain customers despite new competition.

SWOT analysis is not a one-time exercise; it should be revisited regularly to adapt to changing circumstances. The business environment is dynamic, and new opportunities and threats can emerge at any time. By continuously assessing and updating the SWOT analysis, organizations can stay agile and responsive to market conditions.

To implement SWOT analysis effectively, involve a diverse group of stakeholders. Different perspectives can provide a more comprehensive understanding of the factors at play. Encourage open and honest discussions to uncover insights that might be overlooked. Use data and evidence to support findings and avoid assumptions. For example, customer feedback, market research, and financial reports can provide valuable information to inform the analysis.

In addition to strategic planning, SWOT analysis can be applied to specific projects or decisions. For instance, before launching a new product, a company can use SWOT analysis to assess its potential success. By evaluating the product's strengths, weaknesses, opportunities, and threats, the company can make informed decisions and develop strategies to maximize its chances of success. This targeted application of SWOT analysis ensures that decisions are well-considered and aligned with the organization's overall strategy.

SWOT analysis also plays a crucial role in competitive analysis. By understanding the strengths and weaknesses of competitors, organizations can identify opportunities to differentiate themselves and gain a competitive advantage. For example, if a competitor has a strong online presence but weak customer service, a business can focus on providing exceptional customer support to attract and retain customers. This competitive insight enables organizations to position themselves effectively in the market.

Moreover, SWOT analysis is valuable for personal development and career planning. Individuals can use it to assess their personal strengths, weaknesses, opportunities, and threats. For instance, a professional considering a career change can evaluate their skills (strengths), areas for improvement (weaknesses), industry trends (opportunities), and potential challenges (threats). This self-assessment helps in making informed career decisions and identifying areas for growth and development.

In conclusion, SWOT analysis is a versatile and powerful tool for assessing opportunities and making strategic decisions. By thoroughly examining internal strengths and weaknesses and external opportunities and threats, organizations can develop informed strategies to achieve their goals. Regularly revisiting and updating the analysis ensures that the organization remains agile and responsive to changing conditions. Whether applied to business strategy, project planning, competitive analysis, or personal development, SWOT analysis provides valuable insights that drive success and growth. With a clear understanding of the factors that influence success, organizations and individuals can navigate challenges, seize opportunities, and achieve their full potential.

Effective implementation of SWOT analysis requires a structured approach. Begin by assembling a cross-functional team that includes members from various departments and levels within the organization. This diversity ensures a holistic view of the internal and external factors influencing the business. Each team member should bring unique insights and experiences, contributing to a comprehensive analysis.

Chapter 3

Crafting a Winning Business Plan

Components of a Business Plan

A business plan is a foundational document for any enterprise, whether it's a nascent startup or a well-established company looking to expand. It serves as a roadmap, guiding decisions and strategies that drive the business toward its goals. The key components of a business plan are essential to ensure it is comprehensive, actionable, and persuasive to potential investors, partners, and other stakeholders.

The executive summary is the first and most crucial part of the business plan. Despite its position at the beginning, it is often written last, summarizing the critical points of the entire document. This section should concisely convey the essence of the business—its mission, vision, and the unique value proposition. It should also provide a brief overview of the market opportunity, the business model, and the financial projections. The goal of the executive summary is to capture the reader's interest, making them want to delve deeper into the details of the plan.

Following the executive summary, the business description section delves into the specifics of what the business does. This includes the nature of the business, its products or services, and the problems it aims to solve. It's important to articulate the company's mission and vision statements, as these set the tone for the business's purpose and direction. Additionally, this section should outline the business's objectives and goals, providing a clear understanding of what the business aims to achieve and how it plans to get there.

The market analysis section is where thorough research comes into play. Understanding the market is crucial for any business's success. This section should include an analysis of the industry, target market, and competition. Begin by describing the industry landscape, including its size, growth trends, and key players. Next, identify the target market—who the customers are, what their needs are, and how the business plans to meet those needs. Market segmentation can be particularly useful here, breaking down the target market into specific groups based on demographics, psychographics, or behavior. Competitive analysis is another critical aspect, identifying direct and indirect competitors, their strengths and weaknesses, and how the business differentiates itself.

The organization and management section outlines the business's organizational structure and the team behind it. This includes details about the ownership structure, whether it's a sole proprietorship, partnership, corporation, or limited liability company. It's essential to provide biographies of the key management team, highlighting their experience, skills, and roles within the company. This section should also include an organizational chart that visually represents the hierarchy and relationships between different roles within the business. Demonstrating a strong, capable team instills confidence in potential investors and partners.

In the products or services section, describe in detail what the business offers. This includes the features and benefits of the products or services, as well as any unique selling points that set them apart from the competition. If applicable, discuss the lifecycle of the product, from development to market introduction, growth, maturity, and potential decline. This section should also cover plans for research and development, showcasing how the business intends to innovate and stay ahead in the market. Emphasizing the value proposition here is crucial, explaining why customers would choose these products or services over others.

The marketing and sales strategy section outlines how the business plans to attract and retain customers. Start by describing the overall marketing strategy, including branding, positioning, and messaging.

Detail the marketing mix—product, price, place, and promotion—and how each element will be utilized to reach the target market. Discuss specific marketing tactics such as advertising, social media, public relations, and content marketing. The sales strategy should cover the sales process, sales channels, and sales team structure. It's important to include metrics and key performance indicators (KPIs) that will be used to measure the effectiveness of the marketing and sales efforts.

In the funding request section, if the business plan is being used to seek financing, clearly outline the funding requirements. Specify the amount of funding needed, how it will be used, and the proposed terms. This might include details about equity, debt, or a combination of both. It's important to provide a detailed breakdown of how the funds will be allocated, whether it's for product development, marketing, hiring, or other operational expenses. Transparency and clarity here are vital to gaining the trust of potential investors or lenders.

The financial projections section provides a financial forecast for the business. This typically includes income statements, cash flow statements, and balance sheets for the next three to five years. It's essential to base these projections on realistic assumptions and thorough research. Include a break-even analysis to show when the business expects to become profitable. Sensitivity analysis can also be helpful, demonstrating how changes in key assumptions impact the financial outcomes. This section should also discuss the business's financial strategy, including plans for managing cash flow, debt, and investment.

The appendix is the final section of the business plan, providing supporting documents and additional information that may be relevant. This could include resumes of key team members, product images, legal agreements, market research data, and more. The appendix serves as a reference point for readers who may want to delve deeper into specific areas of the business.

To illustrate the importance and application of these components, consider a hypothetical startup: a tech company developing a new wearable fitness device. The executive summary would introduce the device, its unique features, and the market opportunity it addresses. The business description would detail the company's mission to revolutionize personal fitness tracking and its goals for product development and market penetration.

In the market analysis, the company would explore the growing wearable tech industry, identify fitness enthusiasts as the target market, and analyze competitors like Fitbit and Apple Watch. The organization and management section would highlight the experienced team of engineers and marketers leading the project, backed by an advisory board of industry experts.

The products or services section would describe the wearable device's innovative features, such as real-time health monitoring and personalized fitness coaching. The marketing and sales strategy would outline plans for a crowdfunding campaign, influencer partnerships, and retail distribution. The funding request would specify the amount needed to complete product development and launch, with a detailed allocation of funds.

Financial projections would provide a forecast of revenues and expenses, showing profitability within two years. The appendix might include team resumes, product sketches, patent applications, and detailed market research.

A well-crafted business plan, incorporating these components, serves as a powerful tool to guide a business's journey. It aligns the team, attracts investors, and provides a clear path to achieving the business's vision. Each section plays a critical role in presenting a compelling and comprehensive picture of the business, its potential, and its strategy for success.

The development of a business plan is not a mere formality but a crucial exercise in strategic thinking. It forces the founders to articulate their vision clearly, validate their assumptions, and plan for various scenarios. Each component contributes uniquely to building a robust framework that can adapt to the dynamic business environment.

Market Research and Analysis

Understanding the market is a fundamental step in establishing and growing a successful business. Market research and analysis provide the necessary insights to make informed decisions, anticipate trends, and stay competitive. For beginners, this process can seem daunting, but breaking it down into manageable steps reveals its practicality and importance.

Market research begins with defining the objectives. What do you need to know about the market? Objectives can range from understanding customer needs and preferences to analyzing competitors' strengths and weaknesses. Clear objectives help focus the research and ensure that the results are actionable.

Once objectives are set, the next step is to gather data. This can be done through primary research, such as surveys, interviews, and focus groups, or secondary research, which involves analyzing existing data from industry reports, market studies, and academic papers. Primary research provides direct insights from potential customers, while secondary research offers a broader view of industry trends and competitor activities.

Surveys are a popular method for primary research because they can reach a large audience quickly and cost-effectively. Designing a good survey requires careful consideration of the questions to avoid bias and ensure that the responses are useful. Open-ended questions allow respondents to express their thoughts in detail, providing qualitative data, while closed-ended questions offer quantitative data that is easier to analyze statistically.

Interviews, on the other hand, provide deeper insights through direct interaction. They allow for follow-up questions and a more conversational approach, which can uncover nuances that surveys might miss. Focus groups bring together a small group of people to discuss their opinions on a product or service. The interaction among participants can reveal collective attitudes and perceptions, making focus groups particularly valuable for exploring new ideas and concepts.

Secondary research complements primary research by providing context and background. Industry reports, for example, offer valuable information on market size, growth rates, and key players. Market studies can highlight trends and shifts in consumer behavior, while academic papers often provide theoretical frameworks and models that can be applied to your analysis.

Once data is collected, the analysis begins. This involves organizing the data, identifying patterns, and drawing conclusions. Quantitative data from surveys can be analyzed using statistical methods to identify trends, correlations, and outliers. Qualitative data from interviews and focus groups require thematic analysis, where responses are coded into themes and categories to identify common patterns and insights.

A crucial part of market analysis is understanding the target market. This involves segmentation, which is the process of dividing the broad market into smaller, more manageable groups based on specific criteria such as demographics, psychographics, or behavior. Demographic segmentation includes factors like age, gender, income, and education level. Psychographic segmentation considers lifestyle, values, and interests. Behavioral segmentation looks at purchasing habits, brand loyalty, and usage patterns.

Identifying the target market helps tailor marketing strategies and product offerings to meet the specific needs and preferences of different segments. For example, a company targeting young adults might focus on digital marketing channels like social media and influencer partnerships, whereas a company targeting older adults might prioritize traditional media and direct mail campaigns.

Competitive analysis is another vital aspect of market research. Understanding who your competitors are, what they offer, and how they operate provides insights that can inform your strategy. This involves identifying direct competitors who offer similar products or services, as well as indirect competitors who satisfy the same customer needs in different ways.

Analyzing competitors involves examining their strengths and weaknesses, market positioning, pricing strategies, and marketing tactics. Tools like SWOT analysis (Strengths, Weaknesses, Opportunities, Threats) can help organize this information and identify areas where your business can gain a competitive edge. For instance, if a competitor has a strong brand but weak customer service, your business could focus on providing exceptional customer support to differentiate itself.

Another important aspect of market analysis is identifying market trends. Trends indicate the direction in which the market is moving and can be driven by various factors such as technological advancements, regulatory changes, and shifts in consumer preferences. Keeping abreast of these trends helps businesses adapt and innovate, ensuring they remain relevant and competitive.

Technological trends, for example, can create new opportunities for product development and marketing. The rise of e-commerce and mobile shopping has transformed how businesses reach and engage customers. Regulatory trends, such as changes in data privacy laws, can impact how businesses collect and use consumer data. Social trends, like the growing emphasis on sustainability and ethical consumption, can influence product development and branding strategies.

Understanding these trends involves continuous monitoring and analysis. Subscribing to industry publications, attending conferences, and engaging with thought leaders on social media are effective ways to stay informed. Additionally, tools like Google Trends and social media analytics can provide real-time insights into emerging trends and consumer interests.

Market research and analysis are not one-time activities but ongoing processes. Markets evolve, consumer preferences change, and new competitors emerge. Regularly updating your market research ensures that your business strategies remain aligned with the current market conditions and opportunities.

Consider the story of a small coffee shop looking to expand its reach. The owners conducted market research to understand their current customer base and identify new opportunities. They started with surveys to gather feedback from existing customers and learn about their preferences and satisfaction levels. They also conducted interviews with frequent customers to gain deeper insights into their experiences and expectations.

The research revealed that many customers appreciated the shop's unique blend of coffee and cozy atmosphere but wanted more variety in the menu. It also highlighted a growing interest in organic and ethically sourced products. The owners complemented this primary research with secondary data, analyzing industry reports on coffee trends and competitive analysis of other local coffee shops.

Based on their findings, they decided to introduce a new line of organic and fair-trade coffee, expand their menu with healthy snacks, and enhance their digital presence through social media and a loyalty app. They also identified a nearby neighborhood with a high concentration of their target demographic and planned to open a new location there.

By thoroughly researching and analyzing the market, the coffee shop was able to make informed decisions that aligned with customer needs and market trends. This not only helped them retain existing customers but also attract new ones, ultimately driving growth and success.

In summary, market research and analysis are essential tools for understanding the market, identifying opportunities, and making informed business decisions. By setting clear objectives, gathering and analyzing data, segmenting the target market, analyzing competitors, and identifying trends, businesses can develop strategies that align with market conditions and customer needs. Continuous market research ensures that these strategies remain relevant and effective, driving long-term success and growth.

The coffee shop's experience underscores the importance of adaptability in market research. As they implemented their new strategies, they continued to monitor customer feedback and market trends. This iterative process allowed them to refine their offerings and marketing approaches based on real-time data and evolving consumer preferences.

Financial Projections and Budgeting

Creating financial projections and budgeting are essential skills for anyone starting or managing a business. These tools provide a roadmap for future financial performance and ensure that resources are allocated efficiently. They also help in anticipating potential challenges and making informed decisions. While the concepts can seem complex, breaking them down into manageable steps makes them accessible to beginners.

Financial projections involve estimating future revenue, expenses, and profitability. The process begins with forecasting sales, as revenue is the cornerstone of any financial projection. To forecast sales accurately, you need to consider various factors such as market size, target audience, pricing strategy, and historical sales data if available. For a new business, market research and competitive analysis can provide insights into potential sales volumes.

Once you have an estimate of future sales, the next step is to project expenses. Expenses can be categorized into fixed costs, which remain constant regardless of sales volume (like rent and salaries), and variable costs, which fluctuate with sales (like raw materials and shipping). It's important to be thorough and realistic when estimating expenses to avoid cash flow problems down the line.

Profitability projections come next, calculated by subtracting total expenses from total revenue. This provides a clear picture of expected net income. However, it's also crucial to prepare for different scenarios. Creating best-case, worst-case, and most-likely scenarios helps in understanding potential risks and opportunities. This approach ensures that your business is resilient and adaptable to various market conditions.

Budgeting, on the other hand, involves planning how the business will allocate its resources over a specific period, typically a year. A well-structured budget helps in controlling costs, managing cash flow, and achieving financial goals. It starts with setting clear financial objectives, such as revenue targets, profit margins, or cost reductions. These objectives should be realistic, measurable, and aligned with the overall business strategy.

The next step in budgeting is to list all expected income sources. This includes not only revenue from sales but also any other income such as interest, investments, or grants. Being comprehensive in listing income sources ensures that the budget reflects the full financial picture of the business.

Following income, you need to list all expected expenses. This involves categorizing expenses into various groups such as production costs, administrative expenses, marketing costs, and so on. For each category, you should estimate the amount based on historical data, market conditions, and business plans. It's helpful to break down expenses into monthly or quarterly figures to monitor cash flow more effectively.

Monitoring and adjusting the budget regularly is crucial. A static budget can quickly become obsolete if market conditions change or if the business encounters unexpected expenses or revenue shortfalls. Regularly comparing actual performance against the budget helps in identifying variances and making necessary adjustments. This process, known as variance analysis, involves investigating the reasons behind the differences and taking corrective actions to stay on track.

Cash flow management is another critical aspect of financial projections and budgeting. Cash flow refers to the inflow and outflow of cash in the business. Positive cash flow means that the business has enough cash to cover its expenses, while negative cash flow indicates potential liquidity issues. Creating a cash flow forecast helps in predicting future cash positions and planning for any shortfalls.

To manage cash flow effectively, it's important to monitor the timing of cash inflows and outflows. For example, if you know that a large expense is due in a particular month, you can plan to ensure that enough cash is available to cover it. Delaying non-essential expenses or accelerating receivables can also help in maintaining a healthy cash flow.

A practical example can illustrate the importance of financial projections and budgeting. Consider a small bakery planning to expand its operations. The owner starts by forecasting sales based on current trends and market research. She estimates a 20% increase in sales over the next year due to the introduction of new products and a marketing campaign.

Next, she projects the expenses associated with the expansion. This includes the cost of new equipment, additional staff, increased ingredient purchases, and marketing costs. By comparing the projected revenue with the projected expenses, she calculates the expected profitability and prepares for different scenarios to understand potential risks.

The owner then creates a detailed budget for the next year. She lists all expected income sources, including sales revenue and a small business loan she plans to secure. She categorizes expenses into production costs, marketing expenses, administrative costs, and loan repayments. By breaking down these expenses into monthly figures, she ensures that the budget reflects the seasonal nature of her business.

Throughout the year, the owner monitors actual performance against the budget. She conducts variance analysis to identify any discrepancies and adjusts the budget as needed. When she notices that ingredient costs are higher than expected due to supplier price increases, she looks for alternative suppliers and adjusts her pricing strategy to maintain profitability.

In addition to regular budgeting, the owner also prepares a cash flow forecast. She predicts cash inflows from sales and the loan and plans for cash outflows for expenses and loan repayments. By doing so, she ensures that the bakery maintains a positive cash flow and avoids liquidity issues.

Financial projections and budgeting are not just about numbers; they are about making informed decisions and planning for the future. They provide a framework for setting financial goals, allocating resources, and measuring performance. For beginners, the key is to start simple and gradually build more detailed projections and budgets as the business grows.

In practical terms, the process involves a mix of analytical skills and strategic thinking. It requires careful consideration of various factors that influence revenue and expenses, as well as an understanding of the broader market environment. While it may seem challenging at first, gaining proficiency in financial projections and budgeting can significantly enhance the financial health and stability of a business.

To make the process more manageable, beginners can use templates and financial software that simplify data entry and analysis. These tools often come with built-in formulas and charts that help visualize financial data and track performance. Additionally, seeking advice from financial advisors or mentors can provide valuable insights and guidance.

As with any business skill, practice and experience are key to mastering financial projections and budgeting. Over time, you'll develop a deeper understanding of your business's financial dynamics and become more adept at anticipating and responding to financial challenges. The goal is to create a financial plan that supports sustainable growth and helps you achieve your business objectives.

In conclusion, financial projections and budgeting are essential components of effective business management. They provide a roadmap for future performance, help in allocating resources efficiently, and ensure that the business remains financially healthy. By setting realistic goals, projecting revenue and expenses, monitoring performance, and managing cash flow, beginners can build a strong foundation for long-term success. The ability to adapt and refine these financial tools as the business evolves is crucial in navigating the complexities of the market and achieving sustainable growth.

One critical aspect often overlooked in financial projections and budgeting is the importance of incorporating contingency plans. Businesses operate in an environment of uncertainty, where unexpected events such as economic downturns, supply chain disruptions, or sudden shifts in consumer preferences can impact financial performance. Having a contingency plan helps the business remain resilient and responsive in the face of such challenges.

Strategic Planning

Strategic planning is the cornerstone of building a successful business. It involves defining a company's direction and making decisions on allocating resources to pursue this direction. It's a process that requires foresight, analysis, and alignment with the core values and vision of the organization. At its heart, strategic planning is about setting long-term goals and determining the best ways to achieve them, ensuring that every aspect of the business is geared towards these objectives.

The first step in strategic planning is to clearly define the mission and vision of the organization. The mission statement articulates the purpose of the business, what it stands for, and its core values. It is the foundation upon which all strategic decisions are based. The vision statement, on the other hand, paints a picture of what the organization aspires to become in the future. It provides direction and inspiration, guiding the business towards its long-term goals.

With a clear mission and vision in place, the next step is to conduct a comprehensive analysis of the internal and external environments. This involves assessing the strengths, weaknesses, opportunities, and threats (SWOT analysis) facing the organization. Strengths and weaknesses are internal factors, while opportunities and threats are external factors. This analysis helps identify areas where the business excels, areas that need improvement, potential growth opportunities, and external challenges that could impact the business.

For example, a small tech startup might identify its innovative product as a strength, lack of funding as a weakness, a growing market for its technology as an opportunity, and competition from larger companies as a threat. By understanding these factors, the startup can develop strategies to leverage its strengths, address its weaknesses, capitalize on opportunities, and mitigate threats.

Once the SWOT analysis is completed, the next step is to set specific, measurable, achievable, relevant, and time-bound (SMART) goals. These goals provide a clear roadmap for the organization, outlining what needs to be achieved within a specific timeframe. For instance, a retail company might set a goal to increase online sales by 20% within the next year. This goal is specific (increase online sales), measurable (by 20%), achievable (with the right strategies), relevant (to the company's overall growth objectives), and time-bound (within the next year).

To achieve these goals, strategic initiatives and action plans must be developed. Strategic initiatives are broad, overarching efforts that align with the organization's long-term goals. Action plans are more detailed, outlining the specific steps that need to be taken to implement these initiatives. For example, to increase online sales, the retail company might develop initiatives such as enhancing its e-commerce platform, launching targeted digital marketing campaigns, and improving customer service. The action plans would then detail the specific tasks, timelines, and responsibilities for each initiative.

Effective strategic planning also requires a thorough understanding of the competitive landscape. This involves analyzing competitors to understand their strengths, weaknesses, strategies, and market positions. By studying competitors, a business can identify gaps in the market, potential areas for differentiation, and strategies to gain a competitive advantage. For instance, if competitors are focusing heavily on price competition, a business might differentiate itself by offering superior customer service or unique product features.

Another critical component of strategic planning is resource allocation. This involves determining how to best allocate the organization's resources, including financial, human, and technological resources, to achieve its strategic goals. Resource allocation requires careful consideration of priorities, ensuring that the most critical initiatives receive the necessary support. For example, if a company's strategic goal is to expand into new markets, it might allocate resources towards market research, hiring local talent, and establishing distribution channels in the target markets.

Strategic planning is not a one-time event but an ongoing process that requires regular review and adjustment. As the business environment evolves, the organization's strategies and goals may need to be revised to stay relevant and competitive. This involves monitoring progress towards goals, evaluating the effectiveness of strategies, and making necessary adjustments. Regular strategic reviews ensure that the organization remains agile and responsive to changes in the market, technological advancements, and other external factors.

Moreover, effective communication and involvement of key stakeholders are crucial for successful strategic planning. This includes not only the leadership team but also employees, customers, suppliers, and investors. Engaging stakeholders in the planning process fosters a sense of ownership and commitment, ensuring that everyone is aligned with the organization's strategic direction. For instance, involving employees in the development of strategic initiatives can lead to valuable insights and increased buy-in, making implementation more effective.

In addition to internal communication, external communication is also important. Keeping customers and investors informed about the organization's strategic direction can build trust and confidence. For example, communicating a new product launch or market expansion plans to customers can create excitement and anticipation, while providing investors with updates on strategic progress can reinforce their confidence in the organization's leadership and vision.

One of the common pitfalls in strategic planning is the failure to execute. Even the best-laid plans are worthless if they are not effectively implemented. This is where the importance of strong leadership and management comes into play. Leaders must ensure that strategic plans are translated into actionable tasks and that there is accountability at every level. This involves setting clear expectations, providing the necessary resources and support, and regularly reviewing progress to ensure that the organization stays on track.

Another challenge is maintaining flexibility while staying focused on long-term goals. The business environment is dynamic, and unforeseen changes can impact strategic plans. While it is important to stay committed to long-term goals, it is equally important to be flexible and adaptable. This means being willing to adjust strategies and action plans in response to new information, changing market conditions, or unexpected challenges. For example, a company might need to pivot its strategy if a key market opportunity suddenly becomes less viable due to regulatory changes or economic downturns.

The role of innovation in strategic planning cannot be overstated. In today's fast-paced world, businesses must continuously innovate to stay competitive. This involves not only developing new products and services but also finding innovative ways to improve processes, enhance customer experiences, and create value. Incorporating innovation into the strategic planning process ensures that the organization remains forward-thinking and prepared to seize new opportunities. For instance, a company might invest in research and development to explore emerging technologies that could revolutionize its industry.

Finally, strategic planning should be aligned with the organization's culture and values. A strong alignment between strategy and culture ensures that the strategic plans are not only implemented effectively but also embraced by the entire organization. For example, if a company values sustainability, its strategic plans might include initiatives to reduce its environmental footprint, source sustainable materials, and promote green practices. Aligning strategy with culture creates a cohesive and motivated workforce that is committed to achieving the organization's goals.

In conclusion, strategic planning is a critical process that guides an organization towards its long-term goals. By defining a clear mission and vision, conducting a thorough analysis of the internal and external environments, setting SMART goals, developing strategic initiatives and action plans, understanding the competitive landscape, allocating resources effectively, and maintaining flexibility and innovation, businesses can create robust strategic plans that drive success. Regular review and adjustment, effective communication, strong leadership, and alignment with culture and values are essential for successful implementation. Through strategic planning, organizations can navigate the complexities of the business environment, capitalize on opportunities, and achieve sustainable growth and profitability.

Strategic planning also benefits from incorporating key performance indicators (KPIs) to measure progress and success. KPIs are specific metrics that help track the performance of various aspects of the business, providing tangible evidence of whether the strategic initiatives are working. These indicators should be closely aligned with the strategic goals and provide actionable insights. For instance, if a company's strategic goal is to improve customer satisfaction, relevant KPIs might include customer satisfaction scores, net promoter scores, and the number of customer complaints. Regularly monitoring these KPIs allows the organization to identify areas needing improvement and adjust strategies as necessary.

Presenting Your Business Plan to Investors

Standing in front of a room filled with potential investors can be both exhilarating and nerve-wracking. Presenting your business plan effectively is crucial to securing the funding you need to bring your vision to life. Whether you're pitching to venture capitalists, angel investors, or a room of skeptical bankers, your ability to convey your business idea with clarity and confidence can make all the difference. The goal is to create a compelling narrative that not only captures your audience's interest but also convinces them of your business's potential for success.

Preparation is the foundation of any successful presentation. Begin by thoroughly understanding your business plan inside and out. You should be able to discuss every aspect of your plan without hesitation, from your market analysis to your financial projections. This depth of knowledge will enable you to answer any questions that may arise and demonstrate your commitment and expertise.

Crafting a strong executive summary is essential. This summary should provide a concise overview of your business plan, highlighting key points such as your business concept, target market, competitive advantage, and financial goals. It's often the first thing investors will read, so it needs to be compelling enough to make them want to learn more. Think of it as your elevator pitch – if you only had a few minutes to explain your business, what would you say? Make sure your executive summary captures the essence of your business and sparks curiosity.

Once you have your executive summary, focus on creating a clear and engaging presentation. Use visuals to reinforce your message – slides should complement your verbal presentation, not overwhelm it. Each slide should be clean, uncluttered, and focused on one key point. Use charts, graphs, and images to illustrate your data and make complex information more digestible. Remember, visuals can be powerful tools in helping your audience understand and remember your message.

Your presentation should tell a story. Start by setting the stage with a compelling opening that captures attention. This could be a personal anecdote, a surprising statistic, or a bold statement about the market opportunity. For example, if you're pitching a new healthcare technology, you might start with a story about a patient's struggle with the current system and how your solution could make a difference. This emotional connection can help engage your audience and make your business idea more relatable.

Next, outline the problem your business is addressing and why it matters. Be specific about the pain points your target market is experiencing and provide evidence to support your claims. This could include market research, customer testimonials, or industry reports. For instance, if your business plan involves a new software solution for small businesses, detail the inefficiencies and frustrations these businesses currently face and how your product will solve them.

After establishing the problem, introduce your solution. Clearly explain what your product or service is, how it works, and why it's better than existing alternatives. Highlight your unique selling points and any competitive advantages you have. This is your opportunity to showcase your innovation and demonstrate why your business will succeed where others have failed. Use real-life examples or case studies to illustrate the effectiveness of your solution.

Once you've presented your solution, it's important to validate your business model. This involves explaining how your business will make money. Detail your revenue streams, pricing strategy, and sales channels. Investors need to understand not only that your product is viable but also that it has the potential to be profitable. For example, if you're developing a subscription-based service, outline your pricing tiers, expected customer acquisition costs, and projected lifetime value of a customer.

Financial projections are a critical component of your presentation. Investors will scrutinize these numbers to assess the potential return on their investment. Provide realistic projections based on solid data and clearly explain your assumptions. Include key financial metrics such as revenue forecasts, profit margins, and breakeven analysis. Be prepared to discuss how you arrived at these numbers and what steps you'll take if actual results differ from projections.

Your team is another crucial element that investors will consider. Highlight the key members of your team, their backgrounds, and their roles within the company. Emphasize any relevant experience or expertise that makes your team uniquely qualified to execute the business plan. If you have advisors or mentors with notable credentials, mention them as well. A strong, capable team can significantly boost investor confidence in your business.

Risk assessment and mitigation are also important topics to address. Acknowledge the potential risks your business faces and explain how you plan to mitigate them. This demonstrates that you have a realistic understanding of the challenges ahead and are prepared to handle them. For instance, if market competition is a significant risk, discuss your strategies for differentiating your product and maintaining a competitive edge.

As you conclude your presentation, reiterate the key points of your business plan and make a clear ask. Specify the amount of funding you're seeking and how you plan to use it. Break down the allocation of funds and tie it back to your business objectives. For example, if you're seeking $1 million, explain how much will go towards product development, marketing, hiring, and other key areas. Providing a detailed breakdown helps investors understand the impact of their investment.

Practice is essential for delivering a confident and polished presentation. Rehearse multiple times, both alone and in front of others, to refine your delivery and timing. Anticipate potential questions and prepare thoughtful responses. The more familiar you are with your material, the more confidently you'll be able to present it.

During the presentation, engage with your audience. Make eye contact, use natural gestures, and vary your tone of voice to maintain interest. Be enthusiastic and passionate about your business – your energy can be contagious. Listen carefully to questions and feedback, responding thoughtfully and respectfully. If you don't know the answer to a question, it's better to admit it and offer to follow up later than to provide a vague or incorrect response.

Building rapport with your audience is also important. Investors are more likely to fund entrepreneurs they trust and feel comfortable working with. Be authentic, transparent, and respectful throughout the presentation. Share your vision and invite investors to join you on your journey. Creating a connection can make a lasting impression and increase your chances of securing funding.

Follow up after the presentation with a thank-you note and any additional information requested by the investors. This demonstrates professionalism and keeps the lines of communication open. Be patient and persistent – securing investment can take time, and building relationships is key.

In conclusion, presenting your business plan to investors is a critical step in securing the funding you need to grow your business. By thoroughly preparing, crafting a compelling narrative, and engaging with your audience, you can increase your chances of success. Remember to focus on your business's unique value proposition, validate your business model with solid financial projections, and highlight the strength of your team. Address potential risks and be clear about your funding needs and how the investment will be used. Practice your delivery, engage with your audience, and follow up professionally. With these strategies, you can present your business plan with confidence and make a lasting impression on potential investors.

Persistence and resilience are crucial traits for any entrepreneur seeking investment. It's important to remember that rejection is a common part of the process. Not every investor will see the potential in your business, and that's okay. Use each pitch as a learning opportunity. Gather feedback, refine your presentation, and continue to improve your business plan. Over time, your persistence and dedication will pay off.

Chapter 4

Building Your Brand and Marketing Strategy

Defining Your Brand Identity

Defining your brand identity is a fundamental step in building a successful business. It's not just about choosing a logo or picking a color scheme; it's about crafting a cohesive and compelling narrative that communicates who you are, what you stand for, and what you offer. Your brand identity shapes how customers perceive your business and influences their loyalty and engagement. It requires a deep understanding of your business's core values, mission, and unique selling proposition (USP).

Start by identifying your core values. These are the principles that guide your business decisions and behaviors. They reflect what is important to you and your team, and they should resonate with your target audience. For example, if sustainability is a core value, it should be evident in every aspect of your business, from your product design to your supply chain practices. Core values act as the foundation of your brand identity, providing consistency and direction.

Next, articulate your mission statement. This succinctly outlines your business's purpose and its goals. A strong mission statement is clear, concise, and inspiring. It should convey why your business exists and what you aim to achieve. For instance, if you're launching a health food company, your mission might be to promote wellness and provide nutritious, delicious food options that help people lead healthier lives. Your mission statement not only guides internal decision-making but also communicates your purpose to customers.

Understanding your unique selling proposition (USP) is crucial. Your USP is what differentiates you from competitors and highlights the unique benefits your business offers. It answers the question: why should customers choose you over others? Identify what sets your products or services apart and emphasize these advantages in your branding. For example, if your tech startup offers a software solution that is significantly faster and more user-friendly than existing options, this distinction should be central to your brand identity.

Once you have a clear sense of your core values, mission, and USP, consider your target audience. Understanding who your customers are, what they care about, and how they interact with brands is essential for crafting a relevant brand identity. Conduct market research to gather insights into your audience's demographics, preferences, and behaviors. Create detailed buyer personas that represent your ideal customers, including their needs, challenges, and motivations. This information will help you tailor your brand identity to resonate with your audience effectively.

Visual elements play a significant role in brand identity. Your logo, color scheme, typography, and overall design aesthetic should reflect your brand's personality and values. A well-designed logo is memorable and versatile, working across different mediums and sizes. Your color scheme should evoke the right emotions and associations – for instance, green often conveys health and sustainability, while blue can suggest trust and professionalism. Typography also matters; a modern, clean font might be appropriate for a tech company, while a more traditional script could suit a luxury brand.

Consistency is key in visual branding. All your marketing materials – from your website and social media profiles to your packaging and business cards – should have a cohesive look and feel. This consistency helps build brand recognition and trust. Imagine a customer visiting your website, then seeing an advertisement for your product on social media, and finally encountering your packaging in a store. If all these touchpoints share a unified visual identity, it reinforces your brand and makes a lasting impression.

Your brand voice is another critical component. This is the tone and style of communication you use in all your interactions, from marketing copy to customer service emails. Your brand voice should align with your brand's personality and values. For example, a playful and innovative children's toy company might adopt a fun, friendly tone, while a financial advisory firm might use a more formal and authoritative voice. Define key attributes of your brand voice and provide guidelines to ensure consistency across all channels.

Storytelling is a powerful tool in defining your brand identity. Share the story of your business – how it started, the challenges you've overcome, and the milestones you've achieved. Personal anecdotes and behind-the-scenes glimpses can humanize your brand and create a deeper connection with your audience. For instance, if you founded your company after a personal experience that highlighted a gap in the market, sharing this story can make your brand more relatable and compelling.

Consider the emotional impact of your brand. Successful brands often evoke strong emotions, whether it's joy, trust, excitement, or nostalgia. Think about the emotions you want your customers to feel when they interact with your brand and how you can foster these feelings through your branding elements. For example, a luxury brand might aim to evoke feelings of exclusivity and sophistication, using elegant design and high-quality materials to create this impression.

Your brand's promise is a crucial element of your identity. This is the commitment you make to your customers about what they can expect from your products or services. A clear and compelling brand promise builds trust and sets expectations. For example, a fast-food chain might promise quick service and affordable prices, while a high-end skincare brand might promise scientifically backed, effective products. Ensure that your brand consistently delivers on this promise to build credibility and loyalty.

Customer experience is an extension of your brand identity. Every interaction a customer has with your business – from browsing your website to contacting customer service – should reflect your brand values and reinforce your identity. Pay attention to the details of the customer journey and look for opportunities to enhance the experience. For example, if excellent customer service is a key part of your brand identity, invest in training your team to provide attentive and personalized support.

Evolving your brand identity over time is natural, but it should be done thoughtfully. As your business grows and the market evolves, you may need to refresh your brand to stay relevant. However, any changes should stay true to your core values and mission. Conduct brand audits periodically to assess how well your current identity aligns with your goals and audience. Gather feedback from customers and stakeholders to inform any adjustments.

Lastly, protect your brand identity. Ensure that your brand elements are legally protected through trademarks and copyrights. Monitor how your brand is used by partners, affiliates, and the public to prevent misuse or dilution. Consistently reinforce your brand guidelines internally to maintain a strong and unified identity.

Defining your brand identity is an ongoing process that requires introspection, creativity, and strategic thinking. By clearly articulating your core values, mission, and unique selling proposition, and by consistently applying these elements across all aspects of your business, you can build a strong and memorable brand. This identity will not only attract and retain customers but also differentiate you in a competitive market, paving the way for long-term success.

Your brand identity is not just a static set of guidelines; it's a living, evolving entity that should grow with your business. As you navigate the dynamic landscape of your industry, remain vigilant and proactive in assessing how your brand is perceived. Keep a pulse on market trends, competitor strategies, and customer feedback. This vigilance allows you to adapt and refine your brand identity without losing sight of your foundational principles.

Creating a Unique Value Proposition

A unique value proposition (UVP) is the cornerstone of a successful business strategy. It succinctly communicates why your product or service is different and better than the competition, serving as a powerful tool to attract and retain customers. Crafting an effective UVP requires a deep understanding of your market, your customers, and what makes your offerings stand out. This chapter will guide you through the process of creating a compelling UVP that resonates with your target audience and sets your business apart.

Begin by thoroughly researching your market. Understanding the competitive landscape is crucial. Identify who your competitors are, what they offer, and how they position themselves. Analyze their strengths and weaknesses, paying close attention to customer reviews, feedback, and testimonials. This research will help you pinpoint gaps in the market and opportunities for differentiation. For example, if you discover that customers frequently complain about the poor customer service of a competitor, you might focus on exceptional customer support as a key element of your UVP.

Next, dive deep into understanding your target audience. Your UVP should address their specific needs, desires, and pain points. Create detailed buyer personas that represent different segments of your audience. Include demographic information, behavioral traits, preferences, and challenges. By understanding who your customers are and what they value, you can tailor your UVP to speak directly to them. For instance, if your target audience is environmentally conscious millennials, your UVP might emphasize sustainability and ethical sourcing.

Identify the unique benefits and features of your product or service. What do you offer that competitors do not? This could be anything from superior quality, innovative technology, and exceptional customer service to exclusive features or faster delivery times. Focus on benefits rather than just features. For example, instead of simply stating that your product uses advanced materials, explain how these materials enhance durability and performance, providing long-term value to the customer.

Clarity and simplicity are key when crafting your UVP. It should be easily understood and remembered by your target audience. Avoid jargon and complex language. Instead, use clear, concise, and compelling language that highlights the unique value you provide. A strong UVP can often be communicated in a single sentence. For example, "Get the freshest organic produce delivered to your door within 24 hours" clearly conveys the benefit and uniqueness of the service.

Storytelling can be a powerful tool in your UVP. People connect with stories on an emotional level, making your proposition more relatable and memorable. Share the story of how your product or service came to be, the challenges you faced, and the passion that drives your business. For instance, if you started a skincare line because you struggled to find effective natural products, share that journey. This not only humanizes your brand but also highlights the authenticity and dedication behind your offerings.

Social proof and testimonials can reinforce your UVP. Highlight positive feedback, reviews, and endorsements from satisfied customers. Case studies and success stories can demonstrate the real-world benefits of your product or service. For example, showcasing a testimonial from a customer who saw significant improvements in their skin after using your product adds credibility and reinforces the unique value you provide.

Differentiation is at the heart of a strong UVP. To stand out in a crowded market, you must clearly articulate what makes you different and why that difference matters to your customers. This differentiation could be based on various factors such as price, quality, innovation, customer experience, or social impact. For example, if you offer a budget-friendly option without compromising on quality, emphasize this unique combination in your UVP.

Once you have crafted your UVP, test it with your target audience. Gather feedback to ensure it resonates and effectively communicates your unique value. This could be done through surveys, focus groups, or A/B testing different versions of your UVP on your website or marketing materials. Adjust and refine based on the feedback you receive to ensure your UVP is as compelling and effective as possible.

Integrate your UVP into all aspects of your business. It should be reflected in your marketing messages, website copy, sales pitches, and customer interactions. Consistency is key to reinforcing your unique value and building a strong brand identity. For example, if your UVP emphasizes exceptional customer service, ensure that every touchpoint with your customers, from initial contact to after-sales support, reflects this commitment.

Keep your UVP dynamic and adaptable. As your business evolves and the market changes, your UVP may need to be updated to stay relevant and competitive. Regularly revisit and assess your UVP to ensure it still aligns with your business goals and resonates with your target audience. This ongoing refinement ensures that your unique value proposition remains a powerful tool for attracting and retaining customers.

A compelling UVP not only attracts customers but also guides your overall business strategy. It helps you stay focused on what makes your business unique and valuable, informing product development, marketing strategies, and customer service practices. By clearly defining and communicating your unique value, you can build a strong, differentiated brand that stands out in the market and fosters customer loyalty.

Consider the example of a company that entered the crowded tech accessories market with a UVP focused on sustainability and social impact. They offered phone cases made from recycled materials and committed to planting a tree for every product sold. This UVP resonated with environmentally conscious consumers and helped the company carve out a niche in a competitive market. Their clear, compelling UVP not only attracted customers but also built a loyal community of advocates who shared their values.

Another example is a meal delivery service that differentiated itself with a UVP centered on freshness and speed. They promised to deliver freshly prepared meals within an hour, catering to busy professionals who needed quick, healthy options. This unique value proposition addressed a specific need and set them apart from other meal delivery services that focused on convenience but often sacrificed freshness and quality.

In summary, creating a unique value proposition is a strategic process that involves understanding your market, knowing your customers, identifying your unique benefits, and clearly communicating your value. It requires clarity, simplicity, and differentiation, supported by storytelling and social proof. A compelling UVP is integrated into all aspects of your business and evolves with market changes. By focusing on what makes your business unique and valuable, you can attract and retain customers, build a strong brand, and achieve long-term success.

A robust UVP not only shapes your external communications but also influences your internal operations and company culture. When everyone in your organization understands and believes in your unique value, it fosters a unified direction and purpose. Employees become brand ambassadors, reflecting the UVP in their interactions with customers, partners, and each other. This alignment enhances your brand's authenticity and consistency, crucial elements in building trust and loyalty.

Developing a Marketing Plan

Developing a marketing plan is essential for the success of any business, whether it's a startup or an established enterprise. A well-crafted marketing plan acts as a roadmap, guiding your business towards its goals by outlining strategies to attract and retain customers. This chapter will explore the process of creating an effective marketing plan, covering key components such as market research, target audience identification, setting objectives, and choosing the right marketing channels.

Market research is the foundation of any successful marketing plan. It involves gathering and analyzing data about your industry, competitors, and potential customers. This information helps you understand market trends, customer behavior, and the competitive landscape. Start by identifying your primary competitors and analyzing their strengths and weaknesses. Look at their marketing strategies, product offerings, pricing, and customer feedback. This analysis will help you identify opportunities and threats in the market.

Understanding your target audience is crucial for developing a marketing plan that resonates with potential customers. Create detailed buyer personas that represent different segments of your audience. These personas should include demographic information, such as age, gender, income, and education, as well as psychographic details like interests, values, and lifestyle. By understanding who your customers are and what motivates them, you can tailor your marketing messages to address their specific needs and preferences.

Setting clear and measurable marketing objectives is the next step. These objectives should align with your overall business goals and provide a clear direction for your marketing efforts. Objectives could include increasing brand awareness, generating leads, boosting sales, or expanding into new markets. Make sure your objectives are SMART: Specific, Measurable, Achievable, Relevant, and Time-bound. For example, instead of setting a vague goal like "increase sales," aim for "increase online sales by 20% in the next six months."

Choosing the right marketing channels is critical for reaching your target audience effectively. There are numerous channels available, including digital platforms like social media, email, and search engines, as well as traditional media such as print, radio, and television. Consider where your target audience spends their time and what types of content they consume. For instance, if your audience is primarily young adults, social media platforms like Instagram and TikTok might be more effective than traditional media.

Content marketing is a powerful tool for engaging with your audience and building brand authority. Create valuable, relevant, and consistent content that addresses your audience's pain points and interests. This could include blog posts, videos, infographics, podcasts, and e-books. Focus on providing value rather than promoting your products directly. For example, if you run a fitness business, create content that offers workout tips, healthy recipes, and wellness advice. This positions your brand as a trusted resource and encourages customers to engage with your business.

Search engine optimization (SEO) is essential for increasing your online visibility and attracting organic traffic to your website. Optimize your website and content for relevant keywords that your target audience is likely to search for. This includes on-page SEO elements like meta tags, headings, and internal links, as well as off-page factors such as backlinks from reputable sites. Regularly update your content to keep it fresh and relevant, and consider creating a blog to provide ongoing value to your audience.

Social media marketing allows you to connect with your audience on a personal level and build a community around your brand. Choose the platforms that are most relevant to your audience and create a content calendar to ensure consistent posting. Engage with your followers by responding to comments, messages, and mentions. Use social media analytics to track your performance and adjust your strategy based on what works best. For example, if you notice that video content performs better than static images, focus more on creating engaging videos.

Email marketing is an effective way to nurture leads and build relationships with your customers. Create an email list by offering valuable incentives like discounts, free resources, or exclusive content. Segment your list based on customer behavior, preferences, and demographics to deliver personalized content. Craft compelling subject lines and provide valuable content in your emails to keep your audience engaged. Regularly analyze your email performance metrics, such as open rates, click-through rates, and conversions, to refine your strategy.

Paid advertising can amplify your marketing efforts and reach a larger audience. Consider using pay-per-click (PPC) ads on search engines, social media ads, or display ads on relevant websites. Set a budget and use targeting options to reach your desired audience. Monitor your ad performance and adjust your campaigns to optimize your return on investment (ROI). For instance, if you notice that certain keywords or demographics yield better results, allocate more budget to those areas.

Public relations (PR) and influencer marketing can enhance your brand's credibility and reach. Develop relationships with journalists, bloggers, and influencers in your industry to gain media coverage and endorsements. Craft compelling press releases and pitch stories that highlight your brand's unique value. Collaborate with influencers who align with your brand values and have a genuine connection with their audience. Influencer partnerships can boost your brand's visibility and credibility, especially among niche audiences.

Measuring and analyzing your marketing performance is crucial for continuous improvement. Use analytics tools to track key metrics such as website traffic, conversion rates, social media engagement, and ROI. Regularly review your performance against your objectives and adjust your strategies accordingly. For example, if a particular marketing channel is not delivering the expected results, consider reallocating your budget to more effective channels. Continuous monitoring and optimization ensure that your marketing efforts remain effective and aligned with your business goals.

A comprehensive marketing plan also includes a budget and timeline. Allocate resources to different marketing activities based on their priority and potential impact. Create a timeline that outlines key milestones and deadlines for your marketing initiatives. This ensures that your marketing efforts are well-coordinated and aligned with your overall business strategy. Regularly review your budget and timeline to ensure you stay on track and make adjustments as needed.

Consider the example of a small e-commerce business selling handmade jewelry. To develop their marketing plan, they start with market research, identifying competitors and analyzing customer feedback. They create buyer personas representing different segments, such as young professionals and gift buyers. Their objectives include increasing website traffic by 30% and boosting online sales by 20% in the next six months. They choose digital marketing channels like Instagram, Pinterest, and email marketing to reach their audience. Their content strategy includes blog posts on jewelry trends, styling tips, and behind-the-scenes looks at the creation process. They optimize their website for SEO and run targeted social media ads to drive traffic. By regularly measuring their performance and adjusting their strategies, they effectively grow their brand and achieve their marketing objectives.

In conclusion, developing a marketing plan is a strategic process that involves market research, understanding your target audience, setting clear objectives, and choosing the right channels. It requires a blend of creativity and analysis, as well as continuous monitoring and optimization. By following these steps, you can create a marketing plan that drives growth, builds brand awareness, and fosters long-term customer relationships.

Effective marketing planning doesn't end with the initial execution. Post-launch, it's paramount to continuously evaluate and refine your strategies to ensure sustained success and adaptability in an ever-changing market. This iterative process allows you to stay responsive to market dynamics, customer feedback, and emerging trends, thus safeguarding your competitive edge.

Leveraging Digital Marketing

Digital marketing has revolutionized the way businesses connect with their audiences, allowing for more precise targeting, real-time engagement, and measurable results. For beginners, leveraging digital marketing effectively involves understanding its core components and how to integrate them into a cohesive strategy. This chapter delves into essential aspects of digital marketing, offering practical advice and actionable steps to build a robust online presence.

The foundation of digital marketing lies in understanding your audience. Begin by creating detailed buyer personas, which are fictional representations of your ideal customers. These personas should include demographic information such as age, gender, income, and location, as well as psychographic details like interests, behaviors, and values. By understanding who your customers are and what motivates them, you can tailor your marketing efforts to resonate with their specific needs and preferences.

A crucial element of digital marketing is search engine optimization (SEO). SEO involves optimizing your website and content to rank higher in search engine results pages (SERPs), thus increasing organic traffic. Start with keyword research to identify the terms and phrases your potential customers are searching for. Tools like Google Keyword Planner or Ahrefs can help you find relevant keywords. Once you have a list of keywords, incorporate them naturally into your website content, including titles, headings, meta descriptions, and body text. Ensure your website is mobile-friendly, has fast loading times, and provides a good user experience, as these factors also influence your SEO rankings.

Content marketing is another powerful aspect of digital marketing. By creating and distributing valuable, relevant, and consistent content, you can attract and engage your target audience. Your content can take various forms, such as blog posts, videos, infographics, podcasts, and social media updates. Focus on addressing your audience's pain points and providing solutions or insights that are useful to them. For example, if you run a fitness business, you could create content on workout routines, nutrition tips, and wellness advice. Consistently publishing high-quality content helps establish your brand as an authority in your industry and builds trust with your audience.

Social media marketing allows you to connect with your audience on platforms where they spend a significant amount of time. Choose the social media channels that are most relevant to your audience. For instance, if you are targeting young adults, platforms like Instagram and TikTok might be more effective than LinkedIn or Facebook. Develop a content calendar to plan and schedule your posts, ensuring a consistent presence. Engage with your followers by responding to comments, messages, and mentions, and use social media analytics to track your performance and adjust your strategy as needed. Running social media ads can also help you reach a broader audience and achieve specific marketing goals, such as driving traffic to your website or increasing sales.

Email marketing is an effective way to nurture relationships with your audience and drive conversions. Build an email list by offering incentives such as discounts, exclusive content, or free resources. Segment your email list based on factors like customer behavior, preferences, and demographics to deliver personalized content. Craft compelling subject lines to increase your open rates and provide valuable content in your emails to keep your audience engaged. For example, you could send newsletters with updates on your latest products, special promotions, or industry news. Regularly analyze your email campaign metrics, such as open rates, click-through rates, and conversion rates, to refine your strategy and improve your results.

Pay-per-click (PPC) advertising is a digital marketing strategy where you pay a fee each time one of your ads is clicked. PPC ads can appear on search engines, social media platforms, and other websites. Google Ads is one of the most popular PPC platforms, allowing you to bid on keywords and display your ads in search results. When setting up a PPC campaign, choose relevant keywords, create compelling ad copy, and design engaging landing pages that match the intent of your ads. Monitor your campaigns closely to track their performance and make adjustments to optimize your return on investment (ROI).

Influencer marketing leverages the reach and credibility of influencers to promote your brand. Identify influencers who align with your brand values and have an engaged following within your target audience. Collaborate with influencers on content that highlights your products or services, such as sponsored posts, reviews, or giveaways. Influencer partnerships can help you reach new audiences and build trust through authentic endorsements. Ensure that your agreements with influencers are clear and that the content they create complies with advertising regulations and guidelines.

Analytics and data-driven decision-making are essential for optimizing your digital marketing efforts. Use tools like Google Analytics to track key metrics such as website traffic, user behavior, and conversion rates. Set up goals and conversion tracking to measure the effectiveness of your marketing campaigns in achieving your objectives. Regularly review your analytics data to identify trends, strengths, and areas for improvement. For example, if you notice that a particular blog post is driving significant traffic and conversions, consider creating more content on similar topics.

Remarketing, also known as retargeting, is a strategy that involves showing ads to users who have previously visited your website or interacted with your content. Remarketing helps keep your brand top-of-mind and encourages users to return and complete desired actions, such as making a purchase or filling out a contact form. Set up remarketing campaigns through platforms like Google Ads or Facebook Ads, and create tailored ads that address the interests and behaviors of your audience. For example, if a user viewed a specific product on your website but did not purchase it, you could show them ads featuring that product with a special offer.

Building a strong online reputation is vital for long-term success in digital marketing. Encourage satisfied customers to leave positive reviews on platforms like Google My Business, Yelp, and social media. Respond to reviews, both positive and negative, to show that you value customer feedback and are committed to improving your products or services. Addressing negative reviews professionally and promptly can help mitigate their impact and demonstrate your dedication to customer satisfaction.

To maximize the effectiveness of your digital marketing efforts, consider integrating multiple channels and strategies into a cohesive plan. For instance, you could use SEO to drive organic traffic to your website, create engaging content to keep visitors interested, leverage social media to promote that content, and use email marketing to nurture leads and drive conversions. By combining different tactics, you can create a more comprehensive and effective marketing strategy.

Staying updated with the latest trends and best practices in digital marketing is crucial for maintaining a competitive edge. Follow industry blogs, attend webinars and conferences, and participate in online communities to learn from experts and peers. Continuously experimenting with new strategies and tools can help you discover what works best for your business and keep your marketing efforts fresh and effective.

In conclusion, leveraging digital marketing involves a multifaceted approach that integrates various strategies and channels to reach and engage your target audience. By understanding your audience, optimizing your online presence, creating valuable content, and utilizing data-driven insights, you can build a successful digital marketing strategy that drives growth and achieves your business goals.

As your digital marketing efforts mature, it's important to refine your strategies based on performance data and market feedback. This iterative process allows you to continuously improve and adapt to changing conditions, ensuring that your marketing remains effective and aligned with your business objectives.

Building Customer Loyalty

Customer loyalty is the cornerstone of long-term business success. When customers repeatedly choose your brand over competitors, they become valuable assets, driving sustained revenue and acting as advocates. Building customer loyalty involves more than just delivering a good product or service; it requires creating meaningful connections and consistently exceeding expectations. Here's how to cultivate and maintain customer loyalty effectively.

Understanding your customers is the first step in building loyalty. Start by gathering and analyzing data on customer behavior, preferences, and feedback. This information can be collected through surveys, social media interactions, purchase histories, and customer service interactions. By creating detailed customer profiles, you can tailor your marketing efforts and service delivery to meet their specific needs. For example, if data shows that a significant portion of your customers values eco-friendly practices, emphasize your sustainability efforts in your marketing campaigns and product offerings.

Consistent communication is crucial for nurturing customer relationships. Develop a communication strategy that includes regular touchpoints through various channels such as email newsletters, social media updates, and personalized messages. Keep your customers informed about new products, special offers, and company news. However, communication should not be one-sided. Encourage feedback and actively listen to your customers. Implementing a system for collecting and responding to feedback shows that you value their opinions and are committed to continuous improvement.

Providing exceptional customer service is a fundamental aspect of building loyalty. Train your customer service team to handle inquiries and complaints with empathy, efficiency, and professionalism. Ensure that your customers can easily reach you through multiple channels, including phone, email, live chat, and social media. Resolving issues quickly and satisfactorily can turn a negative experience into a positive one, reinforcing your commitment to customer satisfaction. Moreover, consider offering proactive customer service by anticipating common issues and addressing them before they escalate.

Rewarding loyal customers is an effective way to show appreciation and encourage repeat business. Implement a loyalty program that offers incentives such as discounts, exclusive offers, and early access to new products. For instance, a points-based system where customers earn rewards for purchases and engagements can be highly motivating. Tailor your rewards to align with your customers' preferences and values. If you run a bookstore, for example, offering signed copies or invitations to author events can be more appealing than generic discounts.

Personalization plays a significant role in creating memorable customer experiences. Use the data you've collected to personalize interactions and offers. Address customers by their names in communications, recommend products based on their purchase history, and celebrate milestones such as birthdays or anniversaries with special offers. Personalized experiences make customers feel valued and understood, fostering a deeper emotional connection with your brand.

Building a community around your brand can also enhance customer loyalty. Create platforms where your customers can connect with each other and with your brand. This could be through social media groups, online forums, or in-person events. Encouraging user-generated content, such as reviews, testimonials, and social media posts, can also foster a sense of community. When customers feel like they are part of a larger group with shared interests and values, their loyalty to your brand strengthens.

Transparency and trust are critical components of customer loyalty. Be honest about your products, services, and business practices. If you make a mistake, admit it and take corrective action promptly. Transparency about pricing, product sourcing, and company values can build trust and credibility. For example, if your company prides itself on ethical sourcing, provide detailed information about your supply chain and the standards you adhere to. Customers are more likely to remain loyal to brands they trust and respect.

Innovating and evolving your offerings is essential to keep customers engaged. Regularly update your products and services to meet changing customer needs and market trends. Solicit customer input during the development process to ensure that your innovations align with their expectations. By demonstrating a commitment to continuous improvement and staying relevant, you can maintain customer interest and loyalty over time.

Employee engagement is another key factor in building customer loyalty. Happy and motivated employees are more likely to deliver exceptional customer experiences. Invest in your staff by providing training, development opportunities, and a positive work environment. Recognize and reward employees who go above and beyond in serving customers. When your employees are enthusiastic and engaged, it reflects positively on your brand and enhances customer satisfaction.

Measuring and analyzing customer loyalty is crucial for understanding the effectiveness of your strategies and identifying areas for improvement. Use metrics such as repeat purchase rate, customer lifetime value, and Net Promoter Score (NPS) to gauge loyalty. Regularly review these metrics and gather qualitative feedback to gain insights into customer perceptions and experiences. Use this information to refine your loyalty-building efforts and address any issues that may arise.

In addition to these strategies, consider the broader impact your brand has on society and the environment. Increasingly, customers are loyal to brands that demonstrate social responsibility and ethical practices. Engage in corporate social responsibility (CSR) initiatives that align with your brand values and resonate with your customers. Whether it's supporting local communities, reducing your environmental footprint, or promoting diversity and inclusion, showing that your brand is committed to making a positive difference can enhance customer loyalty.

Storytelling is a powerful tool for building emotional connections with your customers. Share stories about your brand's history, mission, and the people behind it. Highlight customer success stories and testimonials to showcase the real-life impact of your products or services. Authentic and relatable stories can humanize your brand and create a deeper bond with your audience.

Lastly, never underestimate the power of surprise and delight. Unexpected gestures of appreciation can leave a lasting impression on your customers. This could be as simple as a handwritten thank-you note, a small freebie with their order, or an unexpected upgrade. These small acts of kindness can create positive memories and reinforce customers' emotional connection to your brand.

Building customer loyalty is an ongoing process that requires dedication, empathy, and strategic thinking. By understanding your customers, maintaining consistent communication, providing exceptional service, and continuously evolving, you can foster strong, lasting relationships that drive long-term success. Remember, loyal customers not only contribute to your revenue but also become advocates who promote your brand through word-of-mouth, amplifying your marketing efforts and attracting new customers.

To deepen customer loyalty, it's also important to focus on creating seamless and enjoyable experiences across all touchpoints. This means ensuring that every interaction a customer has with your brand, whether online or offline, is smooth, intuitive, and pleasant.

Start by optimizing your website for ease of use, ensuring it is mobile-friendly, loads quickly, and has a straightforward navigation system. A well-designed website can significantly enhance the user experience, making it easier for customers to find what they are looking for and complete their purchases.